DATE DUE

APR 0 8 2006		
GAYLORD		PRINTED IN U.S.A.

UPHILL
BOTH WAYS
Hiking Colorado's High Country

By

ROBERT L. BROWN

The CAXTON PRINTERS, Ltd.
Caldwell, Idaho
1989

First printing June, 1976
Second printing September, 1978
Third printing July, 1989

Library of Congress Cataloging in Publication Data

Brown, Robert Leaman, 1921-
    Uphill both ways.

    1. Colorado — Description and travel — 1951 — Tours.
2. Hiking — Colorado. 3. Trails — Colorado. 4. Rocky
Mountains. I. Title.
F782.R6B86   917.88′04′3   73-83111
ISBN 0-87004-249-1

Printed and Bound in the United States of America by
The CAXTON PRINTERS, Ltd.
Caldwell, Idaho 83605
151767

For Marshall,
who has climbed more of the big ones
than his parents.

୭

PREFACE

ABOUT TEN YEARS have elapsed since serious
work began on the preparation of this book. Hiking and mountain climbing have been long-time
family hobbies. The source of the title is nebu-
lous. It has been adopted from a popular admoni-
tion among Colorado hikers who sometimes ask
visitors using our trails, "Don't you know that all
trails in Colorado are uphill both ways?" We have
heard Louisa Ward Arps use this expression and
have found it to be a popular adage in the Colorado Mountain Club.

After considering several possible approaches, an alphabetical organization by areas
was chosen for convenience. Several sources of
information have been used to reinforce research and for cross checking of facts. Among
them are the trip records from the library of the
Colorado Mountain Club, the Library of the
State Historical Society of Colorado under the
able direction of Mrs. Enid Thompson, and the
Western History Department of the Denver Public Library, where we were graciously helped by
Mrs. Alys Freeze and her resourceful staff.
Berta and Bill Anderson, co-editors of the very
fine *Trail and Timberline* magazine, and Evelyn

Brown did yeoman service by proofreading and correcting the completed manuscript.

Five books have been consulted more often than any others. These most valuable sources were *High Country Names*, by Louisa Ward Arps and Eleanor Kingery, Sage Books, Chicago, 1972; *Guide to the Colorado Mountains*, by Robert Ormes, Sage Books, Chicago, 1970; *Grip-Sack Guide of Colorado*, by George Crofutt, The Overland Publishing Company, Omaha, 1881; *The Great Gates*, by Marshall Sprague, Little, Brown and Company, Boston, 1964; and *The Fourteeners*, by Perry Eberhart and Philip Schmuk, Sage Books, Chicago, 1970.

Sue Hamilton and Linda Martinez did most of the preliminary typing, and Evelyn Brown typed the final draft. Most of the pictures accompanying the text were taken with a Konica C-35 on Agfachrome film with black and white copy negatives made on Tri-X film. Although nearly all of the photographs used here were taken by the author, the older photographs bear credit lines for their sources. Several of the others were taken by Marshall Brown, Charles Grover, Jack Morison and Don Campbell. We wish to thank all of these agencies and individuals for the use of their fine pictures.

In many of the individual chapters the second person plural pronoun "we" has been widely employed. In all instances this refers to my wife and constant hiking companion for nearly three decades, Evelyn Brown. A preponderant majority of the walks detailed between these covers represent joint outings. Her cooperation, good humor, and enthusiasm for hiking are much appreciated. For more than half of the hikes covered in this volume, Berta and Bill Anderson were also our companions. Other persons who have provided moral strength and good company on one or more uphill treks include Dwight "Mik" De Witt, Diana Brown, Marshall Brown, Francis Rizzari, Jack L. Morison, Ron Ruhoff, and Barbara, Earl, and Mike Boland. To all of these afficionados of the out-of-doors, our sincere thanks, and the thought that it would be fun to start all over again.

R. L. B.

CONTENTS

GROUP SIX

GROUP SEVEN

GROUP EIGHT

ILLUSTRATIONS

MAPS

UPHILL BOTH WAYS

꧁

AN INTRODUCTION TO HIKING

HIKING IS MANKIND'S oldest means of travel. Yet those of us who have rediscovered the pleasures inherent in this activity are constantly besieged with questions. Most of these inquiries can be reduced to one simple word — "Why?" "Why do you walk when you could drive?" "Why don't you get a motor bike — it's faster?" "Why do you like to hike in the hills?" "Why do you climb mountains anyway?" Or, when students see me walking the mile and a half from my home to the school where I teach it seems to puzzle them. Sometimes they ask, "Mr. Brown, why were you walking this morning, can't you afford a car?" And, as any walker can tell you, one of the most difficult problems we face as a minority group involves contriving courteous ways to decline when well-meaning acquaintances stop to inquire if we want a ride. Sometimes we get the feeling that a credibility gap exists when we try to tell them politely that we really do like to walk. One of my co-workers thought about it for a day and then asked if I disliked him, and another made a hasty check of his deodorant.

None of our answers to these "whys" of mountain climbing is as glib as the three old bromides with which hikers have responded to such inquiries for decades. The stock answers, of course, are the following: First, "To see what's on the other side." Second, "Because the mountain is there," or, third, "To get to the top of the hill." The actual reasons that motivate any person to climb mountains, if they are known at all, are apt to be rather personal and, therefore, obscure.

Personally, we think none of these reasons fits. Our own motives for climbing mountains are much simpler, contain no trite answers and no surprises. We climb, first, because we feel a personal need for exercise. Second, because of the pleasure derived from looking at beautiful mountain scenery. Third, because it's fun to photograph unusual high-country vistas. And, finally, walking in the hills provides us with relief from the tensions of the everyday world. After a day of climbing, when one returns home and turns the key in the front door he is at peace with the world. The problems that had blocked the horizon a few hours earlier have shrunk to the ant hills they really were.

In the two-to-three mile an hour world of simple pleasures, one quickly gets away from it all. Mountain tops have an allure all their own. They widen horizons and lift us above the pettiness encountered in the business of everyday living.

Within the last three or four decades, our Federal Government has set aside nearly fifteen million acres in the National Forest Wilderness system. There are few roads and fewer shelters within these regions. There are no beer joints, parking lots, television, amusement parks, or telephones. But there are more than 105,000 miles of plainly marked foot trails, and all are open to the hiker. Our several National Forests in Colorado contain some thirteen thousand miles of byways under their management. Hundreds of other trails exist but are not maintained. Some were freight or stagecoach routes to forgotten nineteenth century lumber camps or ghost mining towns. Others were trails used by prospectors, old railroads, stock trails, or just paths worn by migrating game animals. Descriptive maps of our several wilderness areas are available from most offices of the U.S. Forest Service.

There are a few common-sense rules that most hikers need to follow, with minor variations that depend largely on personal comfort and taste. First of all, travel light. Down filled coats are lighter by far and much warmer than any other type. Many experienced hikers cut towels in half, break handles off toothbrushes or carry soap-impregnated Brillo pads, thus eliminating a dishcloth and a cake of soap. All this is done to save a few ounces, because ounces soon add up to pounds. Likewise, dehydrated foods have come a long way since the lumpy, tasteless scrambled egg days of World War II. They are really quite good and weigh so little.

Second, wear comfortable shoes or boots. Break them in by wearing them around for an hour or so each day. With well made ankle height boots, particularly those of European manufacture, a good break-in procedure may involve pouring a half cup of warm water inside for ten minutes. Allow them to drain for a like time, then wear them around for an hour while they dry and

conform to your feet. With less well made foot-
wear, such a system may result in catastrophe.
Check with your dealer when boots are fitted and
purchased. Sandals and canvas shoes, as hundreds of Colorado's summer visitors can attest,
are totally inadequate. The wearer becomes
painfully aware of every rock on the trail after
the first mile or so.

Third, a comfortable pack, one that fits your
back, is important. Wide shoulder straps are
superior to narrow ones. Thick pads help too. The
size and shape of the pack and the amount you
will carry depends on the length of the trip.
Among the odds and ends that you may wish to
include are such items as a raincoat, sunglasses,
insect repellent, water bottle, compass, needle
and thread, matches, extra socks, camera, maps,
bandaids, aspirin, a four-inch wide elastic ban-
dage, and an extra pair of bootlaces. If you plan
to be out overnight, obviously the pack needs to
be larger and the list of gear grows longer. Heavy
articles should be placed at the top of your pack.
Wear your pack high up on the shoulders. Weight
resting on the small of the back induces fatigue.

Fourth, don't try to hurry, particularly if inexperienced hikers are in your party. A steady,
comfortable pace, easy for the slowest member of
the party, will assure the enjoyment of everyone.
Short rests, while standing up, are another secret of the good hiker. Only the inexperienced sit
while resting or run up trails, and they rarely get
to the top ahead of the person who maintains a
sensible pace. The hiker who maintains a slower
pace is also less tired at the end of the trail.

Finally, stay on the trail to avoid losing your

way. As a precaution, study a good map of the area before you start. To prevent getting lost, concentrate on the terrain around you. As you walk, notice landmarks, the shapes and angles of mountain peaks. If you do get lost, don't panic, backtrack. Know how to use a map and compass to find out where you are. Follow broken branches, bent grass, or the overturned rocks that mark the way by which you got to where you are. Try to remain calm, and avoid walking about aimlessly. Shelter and warmth are more important than food. When you reach a road, trail, or power line, follow it. As a last resort, follow a stream downhill. Most streams lead to civilization — eventually. Build a fire. Use lots of green wood to make a smoggy smudge and attract the attention of fire wardens.

As with any recreational pursuit, there are a few things one should be cautious about. For example, much of the back country within our National Parks and Forests, particularly that lying above timberline, is the fragile, high-elevation tundra where soil is thin. Here plant cover is easily destroyed. Scars left by man heal slowly, if at all. Geologically, only one inch of new topsoil has been formed since the time of Columbus to the present. Thoughtful hikers take pride in leaving little evidence that they were ever there. Each of us should pack his litter out of the wilderness in litter bags.

Historically, at least five American presidents have recognized the values of walking as a means of relaxation or for physical relief from a sedentary job. Abraham Lincoln, despite the muscular discomfort from the Marfan Syn-

drome, which was not even diagnosed as an ill-
ness until thirty-seven years after his death, was
an inveterate walker. His gait has been described by contemporaries as both "bounding"
and "ungainly," but he walked anyway. Thomas
Jefferson enjoyed hiking in the Virginia coun-
tryside and referred to brisk walking as "the best
of all exercises."

The vigorous Theodore Roosevelt engaged in
all sorts of strenuous activities, including long
hikes that exhausted many of his less fit follow-
ers. Harry Truman's early morning walks were a
source of constant worry to Secret Service
agents charged with his protection. Whether he
was at home in Independence, in New York, or in
residence at Washington, early risers saw the
fast-paced Mr. Truman, followed by puffing
agents and the ever present reporters. Like
Theodore Roosevelt, he often lectured his en-
tourage about the therapeutic benefits of walking. Harried reporters referred in print to the
President's "striding gait." But he was forced to
give it up after the attempt on his life. President
Truman didn't stroll, he walked briskly. He was a
"strider." Both Dr. Paul Dudley White and the
American Medical Association's Committee on
Exercise and Physical Fitness endorse striding
or walking at a fast pace as probably the easiest
of the beneficial forms of exercise for most people. Current research seems to indicate an im-
provement in blood circulation and a decrease in
fatigue from striding after a day of work.

The non-conforming Woodrow Wilson preferred to take his exercise late at night, often in
rain. Wilson could not conceive of anyone wanting

to kill him and resented deeply the ever-present Secret Service. One of his biographers felt that the President enjoyed the inconvenience he sometimes caused these men. With no prior notice Wilson would grab a hat and raincoat and hurry out the side door for a long walk around Washington's often moist streets. His bodyguards, caught unaware, were forced to follow, coatless, and usually got drenched. Most presidents since that time have been more considerate. It probably means nothing, but all five of these men's names appear often on historians' lists of our most able chief executives.

Our leg muscles are the biggest and most powerful of the human muscular system. Muscles pump blood to the heart, forcing blood on its return trip through the estimated sixty thousand miles of capillaries and blood vessels in our bodies. Dr. Paul Dudley White feels that a long, brisk walk in the evening is "more helpful than any medication, alcoholic beverage or TV show." Although no one claims that hiking will extend one's life span, daily walking can keep any of us in better condition while we are here.

The hiking trails suggested here by no means represent an exhaustive list of such possibilities in Colorado. Rather, these are suggestions designed to introduce you to the nearly endless number of our mountain trails. Most of these are easy, fairly short climbs, keeping in mind the novice or the person who wants to get out occasionally for a short walk. Some have been selected because of their scenic beauty, others were chosen for their historical interest, a few were included just because they are a lot of fun.

A limited number were put in because they have offered the chance to see wild animals in their natural habitats. Obviously, this latter category is a most uncertain one since the habits of these creatures vary widely.

Because several of the hikes in this book will take you to above timberline ridges, summer electrical storms must be numbered among the hazards. Morning hours are safest, most storms come in the afternoon. If there is a warning, get down below the tree line as quickly as possible. If the storm hits with no warning, and sometimes this occurs, head down for the trees. Barring this, look for a cave, the sheltered side of a rock outcropping, or get under a rock ledge. If you have a climber's nylon rope with you, sit on it or your pack for insulation.

We once encountered static electricity on Mount Democrat that was so intense as to produce a sound like a rapidly operated typewriter. Elevating our arms caused the tempo to accelerate. This is extremely dangerous and allegedly precedes a bolt of lightning. Another time on Grays Peak, static electricity made our hair stand on end. Although hilarious in appearance at the time, sober reflection and hindsight found no humor in this situation. Our best advice where electrical disturbances are concerned is to avoid them at all costs.

If you should be unfortunate enough to experience troubles on winter outings, remember that liquids are more important than food. Dehydration, unlike hunger pangs, gives little warning. Carry plenty of water, or make every effort to secure a supply in an emergency. For emergency rations, candy bars consume little space and their sugar content is an excellent source of quick energy. Down clothing, "fishnet" undershirts, strips of rawhide for repairing snowshoe harnesses, a knife, sunglasses, map and compass, down filled sleeping bag, and a supply of adequately protected matches, should be a part of every winter hiker's emergency kit. Other desirable items, if space in your pack permits, could include a folding saw or double strand wire saw, fish hooks, line, and artificial bait, a whistle, candles, and water purification tablets.

Know the universal signals of distress. The letter "X" formed by crossed limbs on top of the snow, or stamp the snow down to form this symbol. Three noises of any sort are also recognized as distress calls. Three shots, yells, whistles, or whatever would serve to alert a passerby to your problem. Remember to seek shelter among the trees. Avoid dangerous exposure to the elements in open areas unless you hear an airplane or other obvious sound that might mean rescue. Prepare a snow house or dig a snow cave, keeping the interior small to conserve the heat. Keep your mind occupied, don't panic, recite nursery rhymes, railroad timetables, poetry, or whatever seems appropriate. It might be helpful to remember that your head regulates the temperature of your body and that at least three-fourths of all lost body heat is lost around the head and neck. Illogical as it sounds, if your feet are chilling, cover your head with a parka hood, hat, or spare clothing of some sort. If possible, eat sparingly but continue eating.

Very real dangers exist in the pursuit of any

recreational activity, from horseback riding to automobile racing. With hiking, as with any other hobby, one should exercise common sense, forethought, some planning, and routine judgment when problems arise. Hiking, by its very nature, teaches self reliance, offers pleasure, freedom, and rewards unlike those offered by any other activity today.

~~~
ᖇ
~~~

GROUP ONE

APEX TRAIL

As a snowshoe trail for the beginner, few trails offer the flexibility of this one. You can make this a short or a long trek, and the scenery is quite pleasing.

To get there, drive northwest of Black Hawk on State Highway 119 for a mile or so to the Pine Creek Road, a graded route that drops sharply off to the left, down over the bank to the west. Follow this road for five miles to Apex. This road is kept open all winter to ficilitate maintenance of power lines. When you reach this old ghost town, go straight ahead up the hill through the town; do not turn left. Where the road takes a very abrupt switchback to the right, stop and park. The Apex trail goes straight ahead through the gap in the trees.

There are several trails leading off to the north, most of them meeting at the top of the ridge between Colorado Mountain and Dakota Hill. Old maps show a foot trail going through this saddle and down to the Tolland Road, east of Rollinsville, but we have never followed it through. When you reach the saddle, look back to the south and enjoy the view of Mt. Evans, Mt. Bierstadt and the surrounding peaks.

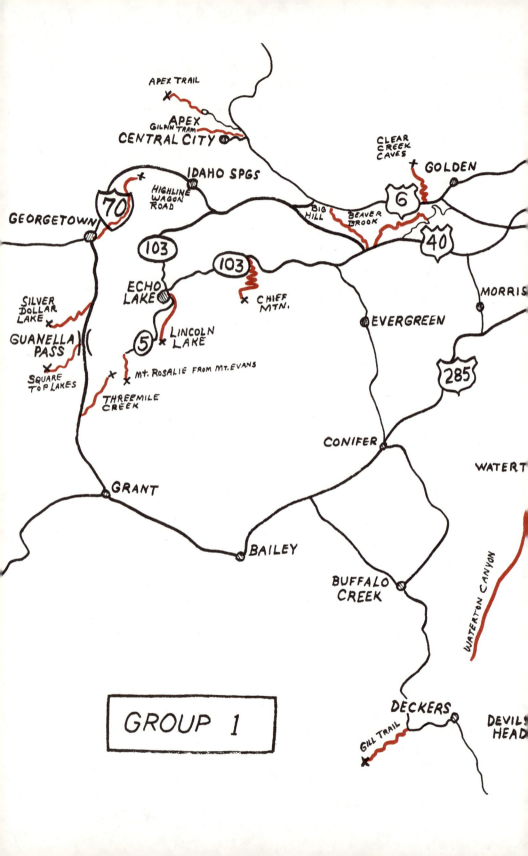

GROUP 1

A section of the Apex Trail, with Mt. Evans in background

From this point we usually go off to the left, into the trees on the gradual slopes of Colorado Mountain, since there is no formal trail here, and merely follow your own tracks on the return. Best season for this trek would be winter, as this is probably too short a walk for a summer hike and because there is no established path.

BEAVER BROOK TRAIL

Historically, this trail is quite old. Indians used parts of it, and stagecoaches once plied their way above its western end. For today's hiker, it has several things to recommend it. First, its elevation is quite low. Second, it is one of the closer trails to the Denver area. Third, it can be hiked in three of the four seasons. Fourth,

On the Beaver Brook in winter

it can be used for just a short walk as well as for longer hikes. And lastly, as of this writing, the Colorado Mountain Club has been active in a program of marking this trail to avoid your getting lost. Although this hike can be started from either end, the easiest way to find it is to drive up the Lookout Mountain road from Golden to the big letter "M," emblazoned on the peak by Colorado School of Mines students many years ago. The swale right beside it is called Windy Saddle, and you will see a small parking area with a foot path leading off to the west. As you hike along watch for the round markers nailed on trees. Some are just tin can lids with the letters "BB" painted on them. Since there are several intersections along the way, these markers are quite important.

Most of the side trails lead down to Clear Creek but getting across it to the highway presents a problem. Further along on the regular trail are several pleasant but not spectacular views. In general, the route follows the curvature of the foothills. Here and there it becomes little more than a cut out ledge. At several points the back of the Mt. Vernon Country Club will be visible on the hillside above.

Where the trail comes to a narrow graded road, if you go left it will take you up the hill into the Mt. Vernon area adjacent to Interstate Highway 70. If you turn right and follow the road down the hill for a short distance, you will soon encounter the Beaver Brook Trail again going off to your left. At the next trail fork, go left. The right branch goes down to Clear Creek. Where the trail enters an open meadow and crosses the stream, the foundations and wooden wreckage are all that remain of the old stagecoach station that once stood on this site.

Here the trail becomes a bit obscure. If you go out of this meadow following the stream up hill, eventually you will arrive at the two bridges that cross Beaver Brook on U.S. 40 at the eastern end of Floyd Hill. People sometimes put a second car here and make this a two car hike.

Another possibility involves following Beaver Brook downhill from the bridge, past the stage stop, on down to Clear Creek. This route will bring you out near tunnel number two on U.S. 6 in Clear Creek Canyon. Wading the creek is necessary at this point, so take a pair of

Overlooking Clear Creek Canyon

tennis shoes and dry clothing for a change after going through the water.

Be very careful; if possible use ropes. The crumbling foundations near the point where you will probably choose to cross are those of the Beaver Brook station and water tower, built and used by the old Colorado Central Railroad.

From the stagecoach station, the alternate trail is a bit obscure. It climbs steeply up out of the bowl by way of a sharp turn around the wall to your left. This trail then climbs abruptly up over the hill and into the lower end of Stapleton Drive, a Denver Mountain Park of uncertain future, currently bisected by Interstate 70. Generally, most of this trail should be passable during late spring as well as in summer and autumn.

BIG HILL WAGON ROAD

Back in the early days of Colorado's mining period, gold seekers who crowded into our mountains did not use the same easy routes that we employ today. For those who sought the great Gregory district in present Gilpin County, there were two trails. The first went west from Golden by way of Golden Gate Canyon. The other was the old Mt. Vernon Wagon Road. It left the valley west of Denver from a point about two miles south of Golden. Here an early town called Apex was built. The townsite was beneath the Magic Mountain Amusement Park, now called Heritage Square.

The road climbed over the mountain by way of the present Mt. Vernon Canyon route, topping the ridge at about 8,000 feet. It then descended Big Hill, rather steeply in places, then continued

A section of the old trail runs in the foreground

Clear Creek Canyon from Big Hill

One of the scarred trees

up the North Branch of Clear Creek to the Gregory Gulch towns. Quite an impressive number of
the gold mills and a great deal of the mining
machinery used in the mountain towns was
hauled over this road in the days prior to construction of the Colorado Central Railroad.

If you decide to try a hike on this very historic
old grade, you will need a pair of rubber boots and
a stout stick. Most spectacular of the sections
still extant is the steep descent down Big Hill. It
is not marked and is not too easy to find. Start by
driving west from Golden by way of the Clear
Creek Canyon road. Go through all three of the
tunnels. Continue on past the Three Brothers,
three large rocks by the creek along the left side

of the road. These rocks were landmarks from railroad days and are now abundantly adorned with trite messages from spray paint cans.

Continue on past the site of the Roscoe gold placer, where an enormous boulder still reposes beside the road and where poles from the gold sluice still protrude from the bank beside the creek. Beyond Roscoe and around the corner a wooden foot bridge spans Clear Creek. Less than a mile beyond this bridge, a very large parking area will be seen adjacent to the left side of the road. Park here and walk up the stream to the end of the traffic guard rail. Now look up the gully across the creek. On the hill to the left you will see a narrow path, apparently a pack trail, although it gets wider and is elaborately cribbed up above. But the old Mt. Vernon Road, the one you want, is on the hill to the right and is visible if you look closely.

How you get across Clear Creek is your own business. There's no good way. Our advice is for you to look, read about it, view our pictures and walk away! But if you are a devoted history enthusiast or a dedicated hiker, you are on your own. The rocks of Clear Creek are like mounds of frozen grease, slippery beyond your worst expectations. The current is quite strong, the depth in late October is about mid-thigh, and its water temperature is cold. A stout stick and hip boots help some. Carry your hiking boots tied around your pack and change on the other shore.

The trail, difficult to follow in places, starts abruptly upward to the west. Where you round the first corner, stand beside the tree and look up the grade. The large evergreen directly ahead has rope scars around its trunk. Don't look too high up; remember that trees grow from the top while the trunk expands its girth. Where the grades were steepest, wagons were eased down by ropes secured by a turn or two around a large tree adjacent to the road. In pioneer days it once took ten men nine days to lower a seven ton boiler down over these grades on Big Hill. Other trees farther up also bear rope scars where their stumps were peeled. Remember that the bark grows back to heal a wound, so look for rope-size depressions, as in the accompanying photograph.

Up around the next corner, extensive rock cribbing held the road on the steep slopes and can still be seen. Higher up on the mountain, after it has entered the trees, the trail is better protected and maintains its original width. A superb example of old, gray-weathered wood cribbing will be found where the trail corners in the gully. Then it gets wider again all the way up to a prettily located open meadow on top of the hill.

Here the trail disappears. But if you cross the meadow to the eroded gully and stay uphill, to the right of the washed-out area, you will soon see the trail again. It now leads around to another wooded valley. Where it starts to gain elevation once more, the well-defined trail stops. Several narrow paths continue on from this point. We have no information to indicate which might once have been the road.

Anyway, this is a pretty lunch stop, and you have now walked just under two miles. Retrace your route back to Clear Creek and return to your car. Although historically fascinating, this will probably never become anyone's favorite trail. Once is enough.

If you must try it, do so only in the late autumn when the volume of water in Clear Creek is down. A winter crossing when the creek is frozen but when little snow reposes on Big Hill has not been tried but might be a possibility.

CHIEF MOUNTAIN

For people living in the immediate Denver area who would like to take a short but very scenic hike, there are few choices that can even begin to approach the beauties of the trail up Chief Mountain. From most places in Denver, we can easily see, and most people can recognize, the flat-topped shape of Squaw Mountain, with a fire lookout station on the crest of its 11,475 foot summit. But few people recognize the higher 11,710 foot Chief Mountain, which is the deceptively smaller-appearing peak just to the left of Squaw Mountain. Between the two, but not visible from Denver, is Papoose Peak, third in the Indian trilogy. There's a fourth nearby too. It is called Warrior Peak.

To get there, take the Squaw Pass road west from Bergen Park. Before reaching the summit you will pass the Squaw Mountain road and the Squaw Pass Picnic Ground. Just a short distance beyond the next bend after the picnic area, watch for the Forest Service marker post on your right with the Chief Mountain sign. Park here. Directly across the road is a steeply cut footpath that will get you up over the cut-away bank. At the top, the well-defined trail is visible. It leads

The well defined Chief Mountain path

gradually upward through a dense growth of evergreens for about a half-mile to the old original Squaw Pass road. Across this grade another and very old sign tells you that Chief Mountain's top is two miles away. Really it's not that far. Continue on up the trail and stop in the first clearing to enjoy the fine panorama of the Front Range. Beyond this point the trail reenters the dense evergreen growth for about three quarters of a mile. Then gradually you begin to emerge above timberline, with beautiful scenery around you in all directions except to the east, where the view is frequently obscured by Denver's smog. To the west and north are the Arapahos and Longs Peak. Turning slightly you

Mt. Evans from top of Chief Mountain

will see Grays and Torreys Peaks looming above Squaw Pass, now far below you.

As the trees grow more sparse, the trail makes more frequent switchbacks, and the rocky top is now in full view. From the summit, Mounts Evans, Epaulet and Rosalie form a massive wall to the southeast. Farther to the south is the familiar profile of Pikes Peak. There are several very pleasant picnic spots to choose from, with plenty of room for large groups. Abundant rock formations provide shelter from wind or rain if it happens to be that sort of day. And when you have had enough of the view and no more film remains in your camera, merely retrace your steps back down the mountain. Heavy winter snows remain here well into June. Summer and early fall are the best seasons for Chief Mountain. Total walking distance is under four miles with a mere 850 feet of elevation gain.

CLEAR CREEK CAVES

This is a very short hike, very steep, and it is included here only because it borders on the unusual. Back in prehistoric times, while the Rocky Mountains were being forced up out of the earth's surface for the second time, volcanic pressure fractured the earth's crust along the weakest areas or faults. Many peculiar features were created by the wrenching action of the earth's crust, including natural caves.

If this type of activity intrigues you, drive west from Golden on U.S. Highway 6. Start up the Clear Creek Canyon Road and go through the first tunnel. The road curves a bit, following the creek, and you will notice two small parking pull-offs on the left side of the road. Pull into the second one diagonally across from the 40 mile per hour sign. This point is less than a quarter of a mile west of the tunnel. Our advice now is to look out the window of your car, toward the west, across the road. That steep, rocky gully that leads not quite straight up is your route. We suggest that you look this gully over carefully, then turn the key and drive home.

But if you must try it, be advised that the footing is most awkward. Some of the rocks are loose, and every step is steeply up. Coming back down is a religious experience, or so it seems from some of the words you may choose to utter during your descent. The cars on the Clear Creek

Entrance to the caves

Highway seem to be directly below you as you
seek out likely footholds. But others have made it
and in places there is a rough suggestion of a
path. Mostly you need to keep going upward toward the large cluster of huge rocks about a
quarter of a mile above the road. The cave entrance has been marked by generous belches
from spray paint cans of several colors. If you
don't find it right away, go on to the next cluster
of granite boulders.

We have been told that these caves go down
deep underground, cross the canyon underneath
the creek and highway, climb up again to
reemerge on the opposite slope. We have not
checked this out. If you choose to do so, take a

light, plenty of spare batteries, a nylon rope and a trusted friend.

DEVILS HEAD

By almost any standard of evaluation, this is one of the easiest and one of the best of the hikes available to beginners who may be trying this hobby for the first time. Drive down the old U.S. 85 south from Denver. Turn west from Sedalia on the Jarre Canyon road, State Highway 67, and go to the intersection of the road to Deckers. Turn left here on the ten mile long graded road to Devils Head campground. Park at the well-marked trail head and start up the path.

This whole trail is within the Pike National Forest. There are no intersections and no ways to get lost. For the first three-quarters of a mile or so you pass through a dense growth of beautiful aspen trees. Then gradually the trail climbs up into the conifers. In all, the distance to the top is just under two miles. Where the trail ends, you'll find picnic tables in a secluded cove next to the ranger's cabin.

Wooden stairs lead up to the top of Devils Head. In summer the station on top is manned, and sometimes womanned, as a fire lookout. Visitors are always welcome in the tower, and the front range view from this point is most impressive.

Try this one in very late spring, for summer hikes, and don't miss it in the fall. This could be a very pleasant snowshoe walk too, since most of the grades are protected by dense groves of trees. But alas, the last ten miles of the road into

Devils Head Trail in autumn

Devils Head, as seen from Southwest Denver

Hikers on the Gill Trail

the campground, a rather exposed stretch of graded road, is not kept open in winter.

GILL TRAIL

This is a short, rather pleasant, low altitude hike involving very little real elevation gain or loss. Inevitably there are some little hills that you go up and down, but nothing serious. Essentially, this is a fisherman's trail, built to provide access to the South Platte River below Cheesman Dam. Since this is a drinking water supply, no bait fishing is permitted; only lures and flies may be used. Most of the hiking trail is well above the river, however, and fishermen just drop down off the side to their favorite holes.

Platte River, near end of the Gill Trail

There are many ways to reach this trail head, located just west of Deckers and the Wigwam Club. All sorts of roads, mostly graded, converge on this region from Sedalia, Pine, Bailey, Colorado Springs, or you name it. There's a small picnic ground and parking area just west of Deckers, with signs pointing to the Gill Trail. If in doubt, merely walk over to the river and begin following its east bank upstream.

In all, this trail parallels the river for about two miles. Up closer to the dam the area becomes very rocky, and the trail is simply nonexistent. If you want to go on to the dam, it's a boulder-hopping proposition. Since summer days tend to get pretty warm down in this canyon, we prefer this walk in spring or fall.

GILPIN TRAM

This unique trail follows a portion of the narrow grade of a most unusual ultraminiture railroad. Even smaller than a regular narrow gauge trains, the Gilpin Tram was completed in 1887 and ran from Black Hawk by way of Chase Gulch to Central City and beyond, serving a large number of producing gold mines along the way. It was almost exclusively a mining railroad. Few passengers were ever hauled. But its close-spaced two foot-gauge-wheels and shorter length enabled it to run along cliff-hanging grades with sharp corners where more conventional locomotives could not have been used.

To get on this trail, go north out of Black Hawk for about a half mile on State Highway 119, the "Peak to Peak" road. Slightly above the highway on the left side you will see the rock-cribbed grade of the Gilpin Tram. At the half mile point you will notice a break in the grade, a mine hole above the break, and a wooden bridge. Cross the bridge, go up the slight hill and park. Scramble up to the old grade and start hiking back toward Black Hawk.

In several places the trail is narrow and has been overgrown by small evergreens since the 1917 abandonment. None of it is steep since the trains could climb only four per cent grades. The trail turns west up Chase Gulch, following the curvature of the hill above the roof tops of Black Hawk. Further up, the trail meets the Chase Gulch road. Cross the road and the stream here and start walking to the east, up the hill on the other side, following the well defined grade. Just before you cross the Casey ridge into Gregory

Western History Dept., Denver Public Library

Train on the Gilpin Tram grade, above Black Hawk

A section of the Gilpin Tram grade, near the start

Gulch, the trail traverses Central City's current
dump, the only unpleasant thing on the trail.
From the summit of the dividing ridge between
the two gulches, pause to look down to the southeast. The ruins of the small community below
you in Packard Gulch was Mountain City, site of
Colorado's first lode gold discovery. Directly
south and slightly below you is Central City.

From this point the old grade has been somewhat obscured by roads. Originally it continued
west to the reservoir, then crossed Prosser and
Nevada Gulches to Spring Gulch, paralleling the
old wagon road to Russell Gulch, then back east
to its ending on Banta Hill. We usually head west
from the Central City viewpoint, choosing one of
the higher prominences for a lunch stop. After-
wards it's downhill almost all the way to the
point where you left the car. From this point the
total walking distance each way is about two
miles. Another possibility involves using two
cars and leaving one at Central City to be used
for the trip back down to Black Hawk. This,
obviously, cuts the walking distance about in
half. A profusion of ticks keeps this from being a
desirable spring hike, but for summer and fall,
it's a short but pleasant walk.

HIGHLINE WAGON ROAD

Through years of disuse, the old Highline
Wagon Road has now deteriorated to a narrow
footpath. In places it is so overgrown that even
pedestrian traffic is difficult. Here and there,
huge evergreens have gown wider than the trail.
But what this trail lacks in convenience, it makes
up in history.

Dating back to the 1890s, this old road was built by J. J. White of Georgetown. It was the main artery between that community and Chinn City, later called Silver Creek. Rich ore from the valuable American Sisters and Joe Reynolds Mines was hauled down to Georgetown for refinement and shipping. Supplies and passengers for Chinn City traveled the road in the other direction.

If history and old trails intrigue you, get off Interstate 25 at the Georgetown exit, cross over Clear Creek on the wooden bridge, then go left, away from the town. Go past the dump and park in the wide spot just before you reach the gate. Close the gate after you and start walking along the trail. Keep left at the first mine and left again at the next trail junction.

Where tree growth is sparse, you get quite a good view of old Empire Pass across the valley. Fine stone cribbing, still adequate, can be seen along the way. Then quite abruptly this ceases to be a good trail. A small pack will catch less on protruding branches than a large one. Since this is a ledge trail, be very careful about your footing.

We do not attempt to follow the Old Highline Road beyond the open point from which you can look down on the Interstate 25 interchanges for Loveland and Berthoud Passes. It is also possible to "bushwhack" down the steep hillside to reach the graded county road visible in the valley below, returning to Georgetown and your car by this route. Total round trip walking distance is about six miles. This trail is now less accessible due to a change in property ownership. Permis-

The trail above Georgetown

Rock cribbing that holds up the trail

sion must be secured from the new owner in Georgetown.

LINCOLN LAKE TRAIL

Have you ever wanted a nice sheltered trail close to the Denver area? This is such a trail. It starts at the Echo Lake Campground, accessible by Highway 103 from Bergen Park or from Idaho Springs at its other end. Park by the Forest Service sign near the entrance to the campground and start walking south along the broad path.

For the first mile the route climbs gently but never gets out of the thick growth of evergreens. Most stretches of the trail are wide enough for two people to walk side by side. The second mile extends gradually downhill and narrows somewhat. At just over two miles you will arrive at Vance Creek and the wooden bridge that crosses it. To the west you can see the Mt. Evans road headed toward Summit Lake. A huge pile of large granite boulders rises toward the east. Its top makes a nice lunch stop and affords a fine view of Chief and Squaw Mountains off to the northeast.

Above Vance Creek the path starts climbing again toward Lincoln Lake. In common with most high altitude water, Lincoln Lake's fishing potential is either sensational or terrible. From the lake you can make a steep uphill climb to the Mt. Evans highway, if prior arrangements have been made for someone to pick you up for the return ride back to the Echo Lake Campground. Otherwise, merely return by the same route.

Summer and autumn are the best seasons for this walk, although the first mile or so up from

On the way to Lincoln Lake

Trail just above the campground

Echo Lake also makes a fair snowshoe trail beginning in mid-December. There are a few sidehill drifts, but otherwise this is a rather pleasant and quite protected trail.

MT. ROSALIE FROM MT. EVANS

In our opinion this is one of the most scenic hikes in Colorado, but there's no trail as such. To get there, drive west from Denver on Interstate 70 or U.S. 40. Then take State Highway 103 through Bergen Park and up Squaw Pass to Echo Lake. From the other end of this same road you can also reach Echo Lake, but from Idaho Springs. From Echo Lake, take the Mt. Evans road up past Summit Lake. Where the road turns right to pass through the saddle between Mt. Evans and Mt. Epaulet, pull off to the left and park in the wide place.

Begin hiking south or left across the tundra. Climb over the twin summits of Mt. Epaulet. The next mountain south of Epaulet is Rosalie. Walk carefully down across the steep boulder field to the broad saddle, then on up the gradual slopes of Rosalie. From Denver, the snowcapped skyline to the left of Mt. Evans is clearly visible, and the hiking route follows this profile almost exactly. Epaulet and Rosalie are the two prominent peaks to the left of Mt. Evans when viewed from Denver.

Rosalie's summit is rocky and broad. A rock cairn represents the actual top. To the east, Denver, its suburbs and the vast expanse of the eastern plains can be seen. South of you the broad, open valley is that of Deer Creek.

Above it, off to the southwest, are Kenosha

Crest of Mt. Epaulet

The author and wife on Mt. Rosalie

Pass and South Park. The Mosquito Range looms up beyond the western edge of South Park. On a clear day you can see the Gore, Ten Mile and Sawatch ranges. Off to the west and northwest are the Mt. of the Holy Cross, Grays, and Torreys Peaks. As you look back at Mt. Evans, the jagged ridge and summit to its left is Mt. Bierstadt, above Guanella Pass.

Depending on how much you wander around, the basic distance to the top of Rosalie and the return to your car is under five miles. Although we have taken this hike in September, July and August are the preferred times. Mt. Rosalie is 13,575 feet high, and Epaulet is almost that high. All of this area is above timberline. Because of these reasons and because there is no established trail, beware of summer storms. Nevertheless, this is still one of Colorado's most scenic short hikes.

SILVER DOLLAR LAKE

This is a gem of a hike, not too far from Denver, fairly short, scenic, and with a not too strenuous elevation gain. To get there you can go west from Denver on U.S. 285, past Bailey to West Geneva Creek. Follow this graded road up over Guanella Pass. As you start down the north side into the South Clear Creek drainage, watch for a dirt road that branches off to the left from a curve of the main road. Drive up this steep, narrow, rocky road for about a half mile to the Silver Dollar Lake trail head.

An alternate route, Interstate 70, goes out of Denver to the west. Get off at Georgetown and take the Green Lake-Guanella Pass road up to

Pretty little Silver Dollar Lake

the aforementioned turnoff. From the parking area the trail climbs up gradually through a sparse evergreen growth. The lake is at timberline. For a better view, hike up the tundra-covered mountain beyond the lake and look back.

Although summer is the best time for this Arapaho National Forest hike, it is usually possible to walk it through the latter part of September, unless there has been an early snow. The round trip distance is under two miles.

SQUARE TOP LAKES

This hike traverses an area on the border between the Pike and Arapaho National Forests. The trail begins at the summit of Guanella Pass,

Square Top Lakes and Mt. Bierstadt

the graded county road that runs across the range between Georgetown and U.S. Highway 285. The top of the Pass is accessible from either of these two places in summer. Near the sign at the crest of the pass, you can leave your car in the small parking area on the west side of the road. From this point the westbound trail, leading off toward the Continental Divide, is clearly visible.

At first the trail leads downhill into a bog. 4-wheel drive vehicles attempting to drive to the lakes frequently get stuck here. Then it begins a gradual easy climb up to the bowl that holds the lakes. All of the terrain traversed by this hike is above timberline tundra, affording no shelter in the event of a storm. Since storms can come up quickly on the Continental Divide, carrying rain gear is probably advisable. Distance to the first lake is about a mile and a quarter. Barely more than another half mile will take you to the second one.

Because of the exposed nature of this terrain, July and August are probably the best times for this hike.

THREEMILE CREEK

This is an easy, sheltered hike that can readily be tailored to whatever length seems appropriate at the time. The grades are easy, the trail is well-defined, and for most of its duration you are surrounded by a modest vegetation growth. There is one brief expanse of open meadow, then you are back in the aspens and evergreens for as far as you may care to walk.

This trail is most accessible from U.S. 285, west of Denver. Drive on beyond Bailey to the Geneva Creek, Guanella Pass road. This is a graded county road that crosses the range to Georgetown. Drive up this road to the trail head, on your right, clearly marked with a U.S. Forest Service sign. Park here in the space provided and start up the trail. This trail necessitates your crossing of Threemile Creek ten times in the first two miles. After that you get tired of counting. In some places there are logs to facilitate crossing. In others, watch your step on the slippery rocks.

Supposedly, this path connects with the Rosalie Trail at a point six miles from the trail head. Mt. Rosalie is not far away and presumably there really is a Rosalie Trail up there somewhere. But people who look for it have not always

The trail up Threemile Creek

In the open meadow, two miles from the trail head

been able to find it. Best times for this hike are summer and autumn.

WATERTON CANYON

Almost alone among the hikes detailed in this book, Waterton Canyon is a year round trail. Its altitude is low, and it is situated in a deep canyon and pretty well protected from inclement weather. Except for bad storms, you can use this trail during most of the winter. Bicycles (new rule, no motor bikes) have discovered this route in recent years too, so you may have company.

To reach this trail, take Colorado Highway 75 southwest from the Denver-Littleton-Englewood area and drive to the end of the road at Waterton, sometimes called Kassler. Waterton belongs to the Denver Water Board, and a treatment facility is maintained here. They also have a parking lot where you can leave your car, and there's a little footpath around the metal gate that keeps cars off this trail.

Originally this was the grade of the Denver, South Park, and Pacific Railroad, a pet project of Governor John Evans, built through here in the late 1870s. Minus the old ties and rails, you will be walking on the railroad grade. The canyon you are in is the South Platte, and the river that is beside the trail, obviously, bears the same name. This is quite a broad trail, and it winds around just enough to keep things interesting. Old bridges cross the river here and there. Most are old wooden railroad types, but there's one very elaborate metal one with overhead suspension features, complete with a date when it was built.

Some of this trail skirts within the edge of the

Pike National Forest. Since trains can only
climb a four per cent grade, the elevation gain
is so gradual that you probably will not even
notice it. The trail ends at the little village of
South Platte, and the distance from Waterton
is about nine miles. Some people leave a car at
each end, walk through the canyon, and then
drive around to pick up the second car.

Ruins of the old town of Strontia Springs
can be seen along the way, and there's one
place were the trail divides. Stay with the river
here. Anyway, the trails come back together up
above. There will be fewer bikes on this trail
during mid-week than on the weekends, a fac-
tor to keep in mind.

Due to projected construction of a new dam,
the Denver Water Board has temporarily
closed this trail.

The river and the rail grade

One of the bridges

BERTHOUD PASS

JONES PASS

EMPIRE PASS X

LOVELAND PASS TRAIL

GEORGETOWN

GRIFFIN TRAIL X

SILVER PLUME

BOULDER LAKE

A.C.G.

9

70

DILLON

LOVELAND PASS

ARGENTINE CENTRAL

TORREYS PK. X

WALDORF

GRAYS PK X

ARGENTINE PASS

GUANELLA PASS

FRISCO

MONTEZUMA

St's JOHN

MT. BIERSTA

WEBSTER PASS X RED CONE

HANDCART PASS

RED CONE TRAIL

HANDCART GULCH

BRECKENRIDGE

GRAN

QUANDARY PK. X

BOREAS PASS

GEORGIA PASS

KENOSHA PASS

91

HOOSIER PASS

JEFFERSON

285

COMO

MT. DEMOCRAT X

ALMA

GROUP 2

FAIRPLAY

§

GROUP TWO

ARGENTINE CENTRAL TRAIL

Just prior to the turn of the century, a mining baron named Edward Wilcox struck it rich in a high, treeless basin southwest of Georgetown. Wilcox was a former minister who switched occupations. He owned most of the town of Waldorf, which suffered from poor transportation facilities. So Wilcox financed construction of a narrow gauge railroad that started down at Silver Plume, switchbacked its way up around and over Leavenworth Mountain and ended on top of Mt. McClellan.

This hike covers only the first three miles of the grade from Silver Plume up to Scenic View, where the railroad went behind the mountain. As you come up the road from Georgetown, towards Silver Plume, the grades on the mountain to the left are those of the Argentine Central. Get off Interstate 25 at Silver Plume and go left immediately under the highway, over to where the road stops against the hill. Now go beyond the chain link fence and walk west, almost to the house. Then cut across to the grade, cribbed with rocks at this point, and start climbing up the hill. Where a choice of route exists, go

Argentine Central Trail in autumn

Snowshoeing on Argentine Central Trail

east. Anyway, you can't get lost on this one since the highway is never out of sight.

Due to a particularly profuse growth of aspens, we think this is an especially desirable hike in the autumn. Because the trail bends around, you get front, side and back-lighted effects with the yellow leaves. Several old buildings along the way afford shelter, if needed. In winter this makes a fair snowshoe trail too.

At Scenic View, once called Scenic View City in railroad days, only empty foundations and the two story fireplace from the old hotel remain. If you wish, you may follow the trail on around the hill beyond Scenic View. It meets the graded county road to Waldorf on a switchback above the turnoff to Green Lake. Obviously this is a possibility for a short two-car hike, putting an automobile at either end and using one to get back to the other.

ARGENTINE PASS

Since it crosses the Continental Divide at an elevation of 13,132 feet above sea level, Argentine Pass is still the highest crossing of the divide on the entire North American continent. In the early days of its use as a wagon and freighting road, it was known both as Sanderson's Pass and as Snake River Pass before it appropriated the name of the nearby but now defunct town of Argentine. One particularly hazardous section spawned snowslides with such regularity that the grade was finally swept off the mountainside. Later crossings of the range, like Loveland, made winter travel and maintenance comparatively easier and caused Argentine's abandonment.

Looking down into Peru Creek from Argentine Pass

Early photo of Argentine Pass

In order to appreciate the best of this beautiful area, you really should do this one as a two car hike. Drive up past the reservoir from Georgetown, then turn right and follow the road to the ghost town of Waldorf. If you have a 4-wheel drive unit you can go on farther. It is easy for such vehicles to reach the crest of Argentine Pass, but under no circumstances should you try to drive down the western side.

The other car should be driven over Loveland Pass, and then left on the Montezuma road. Beyond the bridge turn, left on the road up Peru Creek and go just beyond the site of Argentine, across the creek from the huge old Pennsylvania mill. From this point you can see the grades of Argentine Pass coming down off the peak at the head of the valley. Park here and start hiking up the grade to meet the members of your party who will be hiking down the hill from Waldorf. Have lunch together at the point where your two parties meet, trade car keys, and drive the other person's automobile back to Denver or to some other mutually agreed upon point.

Argentine Pass is a high, above timberline, barren and lonely place. Attempt this one only in summer or on a clear day in early fall. For the rest of the year, forget it.

MT. BIERSTADT

Colorado's Mt. Bierstadt cuts the skyline at an elevation of 14,060 feet above sea level. Among our tallest mountains it ranks thirty-ninth highest. It bears the name of the German-born American painter, Albert Bierstadt, 1830-1902, a Hudson River school artist noted for his canvases of the Rocky Mountains and for the meticulous detail that they always portrayed.

Unlike some of our more lofty and remote peaks, Holy Cross for example, Bierstadt is both accessible and an easy climb. Two possible routes will take you to the summit of 11,669 feet high Guanella Pass. From U.S. Highway 285, drive north of the town of Grant to the Guanella Pass, West Geneva Creek road. Take this graded country road to the top of the pass and park. But we prefer the eleven mile partially paved road from Georgetown up South Clear Creek to the pass. Park in the large clear spots on either the east or west sides of the road. Mt. Bierstadt is now in full view to the southeast.

South of the parking lot is a path down to a small lake. Go around the lake on the south side. The path forks half way between the lake and Scott Gomer Creek. Take the right fork and walk about one city block and cross the creek on large rocks. Follow the ridge to the summit. A few rock cairns along the way, are difficult to see on your return. Locate that small lake and continue downhill toward it.

If a winter climb seems appealing, Bierstadt is a good place to do it. Because of the Cabin Creek power station on Guanella's north slope, this pass is open most of the winter. During our cold months the swamp is frozen, and snow covers the willows. We use snowshoes to get across and continue on them up the peak to the point where the wind has swept the ridge free of snow. Stick the snowshoes in a drift as conspicuously as possible and hike up the ridge as before.

From the top, Grays and Torreys Peaks are prominent on the western horizon. Directly

Grays and Torreys Peaks from Bierstadt summit

Knife Ridge and Mt. Evans from the top

north of you is the rugged but not dangerous
Sawtooth ridge of Bierstadt. To the east are Mt.
Evans, Mt. Epaulet, and Mt.Rosalie, named for
Mrs. Albert Bierstadt. Climbers often traverse
the Sawtooth on the west side and walk the ridge
around for a climb of Mt. Evans. A two car shuttle, with one vehicle left in the parking lot on
Evans, helps. For almost any of Colorado's seasons, the climb up Bierstadt is a scenic and rewarding experience.

BOULDER LAKE

Sir George Gore, an Irish baronet, came west
in 1855, hired the incredibly talented Jim
Bridger as his guide, and proceeded to kill several thousand buffalo, forty grizzlies, and a mul-
titude of unfortunate deer, elk, and antelope.
This "sportsmanlike" slaughter earned his lordship a degree of notoriety, and today's Gore
Range bears his name. One might wonder if the
words "gore" or "gory" originated in connection
with the trail of carnage this man left across
Colorado.

The Gore trail is a very long hiking path that
runs along the front of this range. Its general
elevation is in the 9,000 to 10,000 foot bracket.

There are several points at which one may
gain access to the many trails of the Gore Range.
For the pretty Boulder Lake Trail, take Interstate 70 to the Dillon area. Get off at the Silver-
thorne exit and drive north toward Kremmling
on Colorado Highway 9. Go past the Blue River
Campground to the Boulder Creek Campground
on the west side of the road. Turn almost immediately right by the entrance and take the

Boulder Lake and the trail

Another view of Boulder Lake

graded road across the bridge and back up the
hillside above the campground. Although rocky,
this road is passable all the way to the metal
gate. Park here and start walking.

For the first half mile you will walk along a
Forest Service easement road through private
property that provides access to the Gore Trail.
Rather indistinct signs at two junctions direct
you to the Boulder Lake trail, which is Trail No.
59 in Arapaho National Forest. A variety of conditions prevail here. In places the trail is wide
and clear. Where it seems to end in a hopeless
swamp, back up and go left down through the
willows and you will find the trail again. It
parallels the east side of Boulder Creek at this
point and passes a very pretty waterfall.

Further along, the path is alternately in-
fested with tree roots, slippery when wet, a rock
slide, mud, and lots of deadfall timber that fell or
was placed deliberately across the trail. All
motorized vehicles are banned here and lots and
lots of big logs help to remind the non-readers.
Most grades are modest, and the elevation gain
from your starting point at about 9,200 feet to the
lake is only a few hundred feet. Distance to Boulder Lake is an easy two miles. For a short distance the Gore and Boulder Lake Trails are one
and the same. Then the Boulder Lake Trail
branches off again, and you are soon at your
destination. The lake is quite large and the huge
alphabetically designated peaks of the Gore
range rise sheer above its northwestern shore.
Keller Mountain is the most prominent peak
from this vantage point. A large rockfall up near
the north end makes a fine lunch stop.

If time, weather, and your constitution permit, the trail goes on through heavily wooded country, past two very pretty alpine meadows, both to the left of the trail, and on up into the Gore-Eagles Nest primitive area. One additional mile beyond the lake the trail drops down to parallel the cascading creek. Although the crossing is treacherous, that meadow to the west of the creek is another nice picnic spot, but the trail stays on the east side of the water.

This is a fine hike for summer and early autumn, but the access road would probably eliminate it as an acceptable snowshoe trail.

CLIFFORD GRIFFIN TRAIL

This historic old prospectors' trail was hacked out during the early years of the Silver Plume mining excitement. It starts behind the county garage and switchbacks its way up the southern face of Silver Plume Mountain.

Heneage and Clifford Griffin were brothers from England's Shropshire. They owned the rich 7-30 Mine, so called for its half hour later starting time. Heneage came over first. Clifford followed after the body of his bride-to-be was found the night before they were to have committed matrimony. Although never linked with the murder, he left the country anyway. Clifford was a somewhat melancholy type, and he never quite got over his loss.

Griffin was a musician of sorts too. His leather-lunged friends down in the town used to shout up the titles of request numbers. Griffin, up by the mine, would play them on his violin. One night a shot was heard, instead of the usual

The trail in winter

The Griffin monument

violin music. By the time folks got up there he was dead, probably a suicide. A tomb was hewn out of the granite, and he was buried on the spot, as requested in the "suicide" note found by his body.

This trail leads up to the marker and to Griffin's grave. Several wrong turns are possible, since there is a virtual network of trails on Silver Plume Mountain. A U.S. Geological Survey map is helpful. In general, stay on the most used trail. The marker is high on the mountain, about a mile west of Silver Plume, above the buried site of the old town of Brownsville. Walking distance is under two miles. You will pass several abandoned mines on the way up. When you get to the marker, the mine you see just west of it is the famed 7-30. Rock cribbing and matchstick buildings now mark its site.

Straight down in the canyon below Griffin's grave, you will see what appears to be a tailings dump. Interstate 70 now crosses it. This is the site of Brownsville, buried when the dump of the 7-30 gave way and went slithering down the gulch.

Because this whole trail has a southern exposure, it can usually be hiked successfully in late spring, in summer and in the fall. Since the mountain is steep and the trail is narrow, winter outings up here would not be too pleasant.

MT. DEMOCRAT

Located among the high peaks that surround the northwest end of South Park, 14,148 foot high Mt. Democrat is one of three big peaks that climbers often do in a single day, if they get a really early start.

Looking southwest from top of Mt. Democrat

Top of Fremont Pass from Mt. Democrat

Resting on the summit

Its trail begins at Kite Lake, west of Alma. You get there by driving along the old graded mining road up Buckskin Gulch from Alma. Two miles up this road there was an early town called Buckskin Joe. Beyond it, in the edge of the water, is an old arastra. The road ends at Kite Lake, and there is a small overnight camping facility here if you care to use it.

The trail begins at the lake, well above timberline, and climbs sharply up into a small basin. Watch this trail carefully; it is not as well-defined as some others, and it is easy to lose your way up here. Above the Arctic-Alpine tundra, the path traverses a rocky talus slope and climbs up to a broad saddle between Mt. Cameron and

Mt. Democrat. Pause here to enjoy the view of
Mt. of the Holy Cross and several other well-
known peaks.

From here the trail to the right (north) goes
up over Mt. Cameron to Mt. Lincoln, then around
to Mt. Bross. The trail to Democrat goes left. A
false summit makes it appear that you are close
to the top. But it's not so. There's one more grade
to climb before you reach the summit. The top is
quite rocky, and there is a Colorado Mountain
Club register in a metal tube. Be sure to sign it.
The Gore, Tenmile, Sawatch, Elk, and Mosquito
Ranges are clearly visible from here.

Below you, to the west, is Fremont Pass with
the town of Climax on the top. Beyond it, the
huge, chalky splotch is the Climax dump that
now covers the old town of Robinson. Leadville is
out of sight in the upper reaches of the Arkansas
Valley, some distance to the left of Climax.

Mt. Democrat is 14,148 feet high. The total
walking distance is just over six miles to the top
and return to Kite Lake. But the 2100 feet of
elevation gain makes it seem a lot farther. Summer is really the best season for this climb.

EMPIRE PASS

Once known as Union Pass, this historic old
crossing was once the main wagon road between
Georgetown and Empire. It is also the shortest
and easiest hike in this book.

From Empire a graded auto road runs south
to the top of the pass. But from the Georgetown
side the grade is suitable only for foot traffic. The
short climb begins about a mile north of
Georgetown and is located on the western side of

Approaching top of Empire Pass

the freeway. It parallels the freeway, running generally north as it gains altitude in a single long sweeping grade.

Good examples of rock cribbing are visible along the way. They are still the main support of this trail. Since this involves such a short walk and since the elevation is quite low, one could hike here at almost any time except for a few days of severe winter. From the top, an old mining road goes southwest along Bard Creek and eventually up Democrat Mountain. If you want to expand this hike to a more respectable distance, this latter road offers a possibility.

GEORGIA PASS

Back in Colorado's mining period, prospectors in the Breckenridge district and those from South Park often moved back and forth across the Continental Divide. Their crossings were Hoosier, Boreas, French, and Georgia Passes. Hoosier is now paved, Boreas is open only in summer, while French is all but gone on the eastern side, and Georgia's western approach is a treacherous 4-wheel drive road. Some years ago, work was done on the eastern approach so that cars can drive to the 11,598 foot high top. It is not a good road at all, but it can be driven. However, it is a fine, easy hike.

Start from the town of Jefferson in South Park. Drive northwest from U.S. Highway 285 on the Jefferson Lake-Michigan Creek Road. Do not go off toward Jefferson Lake at the intersection, go straight ahead on the main road. After you cross French Creek there are several turnouts where you may park. Then simply follow the old road to the top, a pretty grassy saddle that presents fine views of South Park, 13,370 foot high Mt. Guyot, and the Summit County country around Dillon Reservoir off to the northwest.

If you decide to go on down the other side, the trail descends by way of the South Fork of the Swan River to Tiger, an old ghost town not far from Breckenridge. Or you can climb up from the pass to the first low hill to the northeast, a lovely spot for lunch. Then hike along the crest of the ridge across the summits of the next two hills. Looking down to your right you can see the road and probably your parked car. Now bushwhack down the hill, cross the old road, watch your step

Mt. Guyot and the old trail ruts

West side of trail, viewed from the top

through the willows and while crossing the creek. Then climb up the gentle incline to the main road and return to your car. A rough estimate of the total walking distance is four miles. Best season for this easy hike is late summer and fall.

GRAYS AND TORREYS PEAKS

Many years ago the Board of Geographic Names passed a ruling against the use of apostrophes to show possession with geographic names. Hence people who prepare accounts like this one are not being ungrammatical when writing the names of mountain peaks in this way. Members of the Colorado Mountain Club add further injury be referring to both of these mountains together by the single polysyllabic term, "Grazentorreys," probably because most climbers do both peaks at the same time.

While these peaks can be climbed from Mt. McClellan, most people drive west from Silver Plume on Interstate 70 to Bakersville. Turn off south (left) up the graded Stevens Gulch road. Just before you reach the Stevens Mine, a sign on the right indicates the Grays Peak Trail. Park here, cross the stream the best way you can and start up the trail. From this point the distance to the summit of Grays is under three miles.

As 14,000 foot high peaks go, these two are among the easiest for the beginner. Grays is 14,274 and Torreys is 14,264 feet high. Both are on the Continental Divide. Actually, the trail goes up Grays and is very well defined all the way to the top. All of it is on the peak's south side. But if the weather starts to turn bad, get down off

Hikers on trail to Grays Peak

these peaks at once. All of this trail is above timberline, and electrical storms come in fast and are absolutely fierce up here. We have survived two storms on these mountains. If you start early and get off the summit before noon, your chances of avoiding storms are somewhat better.

The rectangular rock wall formation on the top of Grays is a good lunch stop. This wall is all that remains of a U.S. Government signal station that once stood here. If you want to climb Torreys too, go back down the trail to the level of the saddle, then cross over and begin climbing. Although no trail as such exists on Torreys, it's easy to see where you need to go and how to

Marshall Brown near top of Grays

Snowslide, saddle between Grays and Torreys

Old signal station, top of Grays Peak

return to the trail. Since your objectives are never out of sight, getting lost here would be nearly impossible.

Summer and early autumn are the preferred times for these peaks. But in recent years enthusiasm for winter mountaineering has been growing. Denver's Junior Colorado Mountain Club has made winter ascents of Grays and Torreys. One of the photographs shows a snowslide running from the saddle between them. And those two specks below and to the left of the slide path are people. "Grazentorreys" are not the places to start your winter mountaineering experiences, however. But as a first "fourteener" in summer, there's hardly a better place to begin. The total elevation gain from Stevens Gulch to the summit is a mere 3,800 feet.

HANDCART GULCH

Civil War history has laid a heavy and compulsive hand on this beautiful high altitude gulch. In 1864 the Confederate Reynolds Gang from Texas staged a last-ditch exercise in desperation when they robbed the Buckskin Coach near Como. Their goal was to capture enough gold and silver to finance the purchase of more munitions for the South. Allegedly, they got $40,000 from the McLoughlin stage station. Following two days of "cops and robbers" with three armed citizens' posses, the harassed guerrillas were driven back up a valley to the north near Kenosha Pass, probably but not certainly Handcart Gulch. The money, buried near the head of the valley following a running fight, has never been found.

Stagecoach road, Webster and Red Cone Peaks

Red Cone from lunch stop at head of trail

In later years the Webster brothers built a
toll road up this valley, crossing the range to
Summit County by way of Webster Pass. With
disuse of the trail, beaver colonies have become
very active, constructing extensive dams that
have all but obliterated the old Webster road in
several places. But foot travel is no problem at
all. Take U.S. 285 to the eastern foot of Kenosha
Pass. Turn north at the old ghost town of Webster and drive to the Hall Valley Campground.

Three trails start here. The left one goes up
Hall Valley, the right one goes up Red Cone. The
middle one will take you up Handcart Gulch. Distance to the head of the valley is just over two
and a half miles. Add another mile if you decide
to hike on up to the top of Webster Pass. The river
that parallels this trail is the North Fork of the
South Platte. An old log cabin stands beside the
trail about a mile above the campground. It belonged to Vernon Crow, a 20th Century miner
who prospected this valley for many years.

Just after you cross the river in the bowl at
the head of the valley, you will find some very
pretty picnic spots among the growth of evergreens just above the trail. From here the zigzag cuts of Webster Pass are clearly visible above
you. The intensely red peak to the right of the
pass is Red Cone.

Best season for this hike is summer, from
mid-June through September. After the first
snow, forget it.

HANDCART PASS

This remote, difficult to find, old 19th century
pack trail was never a popular route, and we

Handcart Pass and Continental Divide

doubt that any handcarts ever got across it. But the name came from the fact that two Norwegians, using handcarts to transport their mining equipment, were the first people who sought precious metals in this beautiful valley. Actually, the name of the pass came from the fact that it connects the upper reaches of Hall Valley with the head of Handcart Gulch.

In the beginning Webster Pass was known as Handcart Pass, but all of that changed after the Webster brothers improved the road. Today's Handcart and Webster passes are separate crossings, although they are not far apart.

To get there, drive up U.S. 285 from Denver to the eastern foot of Kenosha Pass. The cluster of abandoned buildings on your right was the old town of Webster. Turn right here and follow the recommendations on the signs. Quite simply, this isn't the best road in the world. But we have never had trouble here, even with a conventional car. Use caution, however, and remember that conditions vary from year to year.

Go straight on through the Hall Valley picnic ground; don't turn right here. Drive up Hall Valley to the end of the road. The few maps that still show Handcart Pass indicate that it starts up from the end of this road. It doesn't. The road ends at the Whale Mine. But Handcart Pass starts up the ridge to the northeast (right) from a point about a hundred yards or so below the mine. The U.S.G.S. Montezuma quadrangle map shows the pass route correctly but does not label it.

The trail is dim and indistinct and definitely shows signs of little use. You have already gained most of your elevation getting up here on the road, so it's just a short distance up to the top of the ridge. From here on the trail is even more indistinct. It stays up here on the ridge, goes along south of Teller Mountain, between it and Handcart Peak, to the summit of Webster Pass. Before you reach Webster Pass the trail branches left, and this part of it drops down past the Cashier mine to the headwaters of the Snake River and ultimately on down to Montezuma. We wonder which of these routes was the original grade. From the Webster Pass branch you could just retrace your steps back to the car, but there's another possibility too.

You might run this one as a two car hike.

Leave one car back there at the Hall Valley picnic ground. Drive the second up here as previously indicated, and take the hike just described. Then from the top of Webster Pass, turn right from the low saddle, switchback down into Handcart Gulch and follow the ruts of the abandoned 19th century stagecoach road back to Hall Valley and your car.

For best results, try this one in summer or early fall. Because you are above timberline, keep a wary eye out for storms.

JONES PASS

Originally, Jones Pass was a 12,451 foot high wagon road from the eastern slope across the Continental Divide to Middle Park. Since there are now better routes across, Jones Pass has never been paved and receives little in the way of maintenance. For example, in 1971, the last of the snow was cleared off the top during the fourth week of July. So without traffic, this old road makes a pretty nice hike.

From U.S. 40, west of Empire, the road in here turns off to the north, almost at the foot of Berthoud Pass. Drive on past the American Metals Climax workings and park in the broad space on the last curve before timberline. At this point the current road goes right, while the old original trail continues straight ahead. Stay on the old trail as you begin walking. The distance from here to the top is just over two miles. Since you are above timberline, the scenery is very rugged and worth a photograph or two.

Near the top an old trail takes off to the right and goes to the top of the range, probably provid-

Jones Pass in winter

Near top of the pass in late July

ing access to the old Vasquez Pass trail which runs above and to the northeast of Jones Pass. Longs and the Indian Peaks are visible to the north, while the familiar profile of Grays and Torreys Peaks appears on the southern horizon.

In summer, before the plows get through, this makes a rather attractive walk. In winter, since Jones Pass remains closed, snowmobiles use the area. It can also be a rather nice showshoe trail when these vehicles are absent. There is, however, a very real avalanche danger from the high treeless basins, and danger signs are posted in winter. So except for spring, the Jones Pass area can be used year round.

LOVELAND PASS TRAIL

This beautiful hike can best be enjoyed in late summer and early autumn, certainly not later than the first high altitude snow flurry. Since you will be able to follow a visible trail only for the first mile or less, and since you will be walking along the crest of the Continental Divide, some extra prudence is dictated. On the positive side, the paved Loveland Pass highway is clearly in view from most of your route. But vision-obscuring storms can move in quickly at this elevation, so watch it! Total walking distance is about 4¾ miles.

Start by driving to the summit of Loveland Pass and parking in the wide areas along either side of the pavement. Assuming that you approach the pass from the east, the trail starts up from the right side of the road. There's a path from the left too, but it doesn't amount to much. In general your route follows north along the

On the path, mid-June

View of Continental Divide from the trail

divide from the highway. You will gain some elevation in the first mile or so, and in some places you lose altitude too. Generally, stay on the crest of the range.

You will pass well above the Arapaho Basin ski tow, and its upper building and cables can be seen at a distance. Then you will notice a modest grade ahead of you. We climb over this and have lunch on the tundra. There's nowhere else to go, for an abrupt downgrade begins here. Far below are the twisting switchbacks of the eastern approach to Loveland Pass.

The Alpine vistas along this trail are the most compelling reasons for hiking it. Just over the first ridge, snow-crested peaks come into view that are not seen from the highway. As you hike along, new panoramas continue to unfold. Mt. Pettengill to the west and Grays and Torreys to the south, among others. In short, take a camera and more film than you think you'll need.

QUANDARY PEAK

Sporting an elevation of 14,252 feet, Quandary Peak easily qualifies as one of Colorado's "fourteeners." It is generally considered to be one of the easier climbs among our really high mountains. Getting to the trail head is no problem. Drive north from Alma across Hoosier Pass. Turn west (left) on the dirt road that goes up the valley of Monte Cristo Creek, now the site of many new mountain homes. Park near the old stock trail, a path that runs north across Quandary's eastern shoulder.

Hike up this trail to the ridge, still in the timber, and bushwhack uphill. When you emerge from the trees, your route will be clearly apparent and any needed corrections in your direction can be made here. The path up the ridge through the trees is difficult to find, but when you have the peak in view there's no problem.

Once you reach that long ridge, there's a fairly evident footpath all the way to the summit. Off to the northwest, Grays and Torreys are visible. Mt. Silverheels is behind you, across the Hoosier Pass road to the east. And directly south of you are Lincoln, Bross, and Democrat, three more "fourteeners" that can be climbed in a single long day from Kite Lake up Buckskin Gulch.

When you get up above the tundra grasses, the remainder of the route to the summit is mostly rocky. We have never failed to see conys and at least one ptarmigan in this region. Rock cairns mark the trail in some places. There's a deceptive false summit, but the real top is not far away. Sign the Mountain Club roster on the top. It is inside a capped, threaded piece of iron pipe down among the rocks. And don't be alarmed because your signature isn't up to par. Lack of oxygen is the culprit.

In common with most high mountains, the view from the top is spectacular. To the north you can see the edge of Breckenridge in the Blue River Valley and the Tenmile Range. Several intensely blue lakes, called tarns, can be seen in the hanging valleys below you. And to the west, the cleft topped ridge is Notch Mountain. The square topped mountain to its left is the Mt. of the Holy Cross. Curiously, the Continental

Quandary Peak from old cattle trail

Looking back from the top

View to the north from Quandary's summit

Divide runs east to west at a point south of Quandary, not north and south.

We usually figure this hike at eight miles, but we got lost in the timber once and the pedometer said eleven miles by the time we got off the peak and back to the car. Summer and early autumn are the best seasons for a climb up Quandary, although it has been done in the winter.

RED CONE

Red Cone is a beautiful, iron-oxide-impregnated peak that rises 12,806 feet above the head of Handcart Gulch. It is visible to the northeast from the summit of Kenosha Pass. Two climbing routes will put you on its top.

Near the top of Red Cone Peak

Looking down into Handcart Gulch

Use the route described in the Handcart
Gulch chapter to reach the head of the North
Fork of the South Platte River Valley, then ford
the stream and follow the old stagecoach ruts
northeast to the summit of Webster Pass. From
the top, follow the ruts up the rocky hill to your
right and continue on to the crest of Red Cone.

An equally pretty route also originates at the
Hall Valley Campground. Start up the same approach to Handcart Gulch, but take the first fork
that swings back sharply to your right and follow
the 4-wheel drive tracks up through huge stands
of evergreen timber. You might want to stop to
explore around the old log miners' cabins. This
was not a town, just a cluster of buildings.

In places this trail gets pretty steep. It
emerges above timberline and follows the spine
of the ridge around to the northwest. Several
wind-swept grotesquely gnarled trees afford attractive picture possibilities. The snow-covered
peaks to your right (east) are Mt. Evans, Mt.
Epaulet, and Mt. Rosalie. To the west (left), the
huge open area is South Park. Beyond it are the
peaks of the Mosquito Range. Looking off to the
northwest, on a clear day, you can see the Mt. of
the Holy Cross. Since you are above timberline
for much of the time on this hike, beware of electrical storms. Also, this is a rather long hike,
about six or seven miles each way. The best seasons for this trek are summer, July and August,
or early September if there has been no snow in
the high country.

SAINTS JOHN

By all odds, this is our favorite snowshoe trail in Colorado. In summer, Jeeps and some cars go up and down this old mining road, making it an undesirable foot trail. But from mid-December through the end of March, this is a beautiful place.

From the western foot of Loveland Pass, drive up the Snake River road to Montezuma. Go through the town and park in the cleared place where plows have turned around on the right side of the road. Put on your snowshoes and climb up to the top of the drifts, then head across the meadow toward the buildings in the edge of the trees. The trail passes right between these structures, then bends to the right as it climbs up a series of switchbacks over the shoulder of Glacier Mountain.

Where the trail hairpins abruptly left, you have entered the valley of Saints John Creek. The trail stays close to Glacier Mountain. The mine across the valley was the Pickerel. There are bogs under the snow in that attractive open meadow. Despite this, many people snowshoe and ski there. Further up, where tree growth is more sparse, watch for avalanches. Although we have never seen them run here, their paths are evident and old mining records describe them. Back behind you, the two most prominent peaks are Grays and Torreys, both 14,000 footers, and to their left is Lenawee Peak.

Despite the snow depth, the place where the stream crosses the trail is usually evident. Beyond it the trail climbs again and the old buildings come into view. Historically, Saints John

was one of Colorado's earliest silver mining
towns, dating from 1865. Its unusual name came
from the fact that the town was established by a
Masonic group from Boston who named it for the
two patron saints of the Masonic order, John the
Baptist and John the Evangelist, hence the
plural Saints John. Although most of the town
was abandoned after repeal of the Sherman Act
in 1893, some families went on living there well
into the present century.

If it's a pretty day and time permits, you
could go on above the town to the Wild Irishman
Mine. A well-established trail exists all the way
up to the top of Glacier Mountain, but some of it
gets pretty rough toward the end of winter when
heavy winds blow sloping drifts across the trail.
Total distance from Montezuma to Saints John
and return is under four miles. Add another two
miles if you continue up to the Wild Irishman.

Saints John in summer

A winter panorama of the town

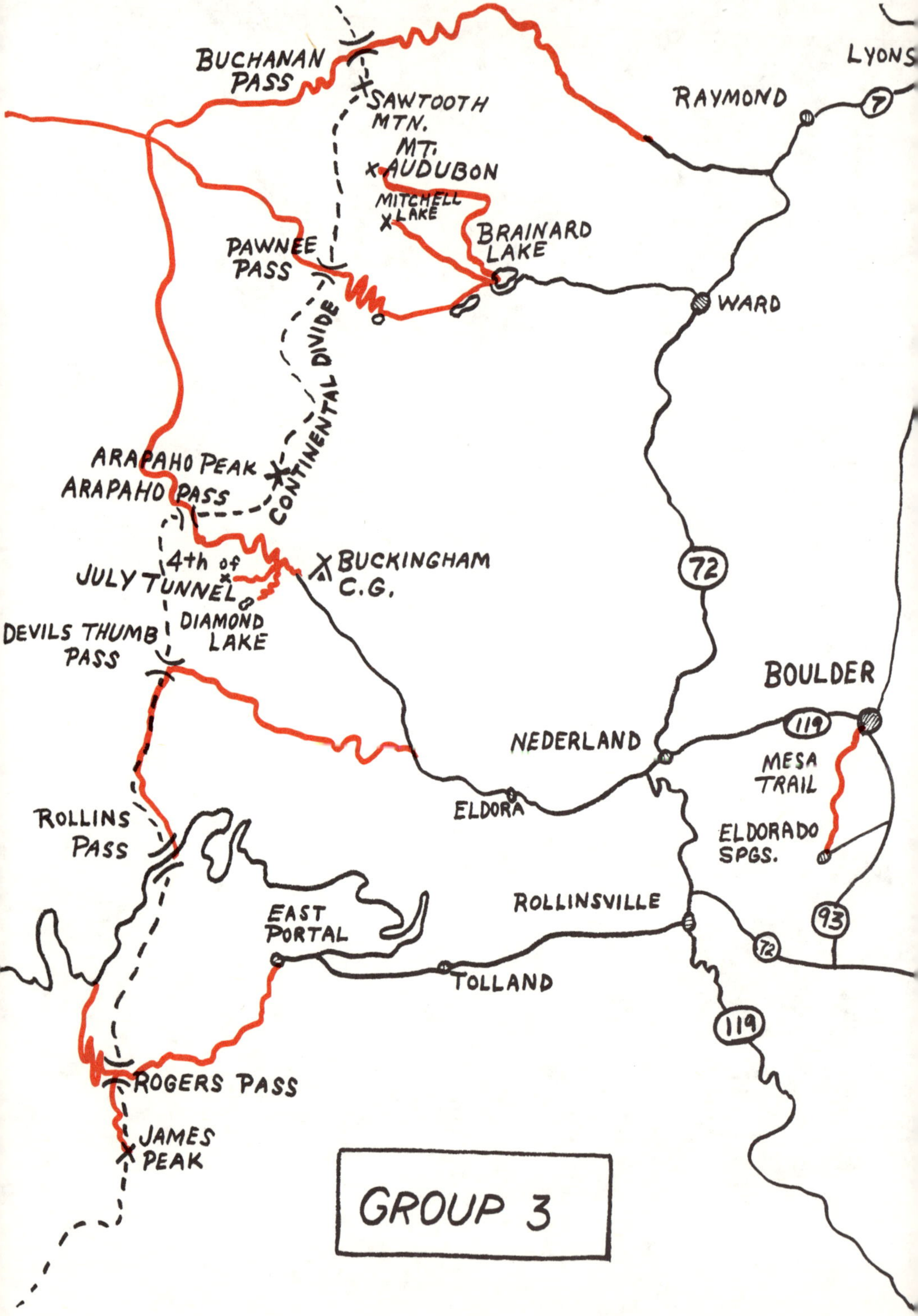

BUCHANAN PASS

LYONS

RAYMOND

7

SAWTOOTH MTN.

MT. AUDUBON

MITCHELL LAKE

BRAINARD LAKE

PAWNEE PASS

WARD

CONTINENTAL DIVIDE

ARAPAHO PEAK
ARAPAHO PASS

72

4th of JULY TUNNEL

BUCKINGHAM C.G.

DEVILS THUMB PASS

DIAMOND LAKE

BOULDER

119

MESA TRAIL

NEDERLAND

ELDORA

ELDORADO SPGS.

ROLLINS PASS

EAST PORTAL

ROLLINSVILLE

93

72

TOLLAND

119

ROGERS PASS

JAMES PEAK

GROUP 3

GROUP THREE

ARAPAHO PASS

By almost any standard, this is one of the widest, best planned and most scenic of Colorado's high mountain trails. Total round trip walking distance is about six miles. In August the blanket of wild flowers that grows beside the path provides an exposure to remarkable beauty.

Start from Eldora, west of State Highway 119, and drive west past the turnoff to Hessie and up the rough five mile road to Buckingham Campground. Park here, duck under the barricade that keeps motorized traffic off this trail, and start up. Keep right at the first two well marked junctions. In general this is a wooded trail for the first mile. Then it begins to emerge into a terrain of sparse growth with pretty views of pointed Mt. Neva to the southwest.

Then, almost at timberline, the path levels out and crosses a high tundra meadow. At the dump and wreckage of the famous old Fourth of July Mine, a side trail turns north to the Arapaho Peak and Glacier, source of Boulder's water supply. But the Arapaho Pass trail goes straight ahead, then climbs up a rocky slope to the Conti-

Early view of Fourth of July Mine

Mine site below Arapaho Pass. Mt. Neva at left

nental Divide and the crest of the 11,906 foot high pass. Pause here for lunch and to enjoy the view.

Originally this trail was a narrow wagon road that zigzagged and doubled back and forth along the steep slope to the Fourth of July Mine. Once there was a road plan to connect Boulder and Grand Counties. Boulder County constructed its share to the summit of Arapaho Pass. But the Grand County grades somehow never evolved. Now, with disuse, the road is just a foot trail.

On the western side, a less spectacular approach, the trail descends Arapaho Creek to Monarch Lake and civilization. A left fork from this point will carry you down Ranch and Strawberry Creeks along a route now called the High Lonesome Trail. It emerges just south of Granby. Best times for this hike are late summer and fall. If time and your endurance permit, you can follow the trail from the summit on to the northwest to the remote Caribou Pass.

MT. AUDUBON

The noted American ornithologist, John James Audubon, 1785-1851, was the source of this mountain's name. It towers more than 13,000 feet high and is located north and west of Brainard Lake. A fine paved road from Ward will take you to the Mitchell Lake parking lot. A trail head for this hike is on the north side of the area.

For most of the first mile or so, the trail is in the shade of dense stands of aspen and evergreen trees. The path is wide and not particularly steep. Where it starts to gain altitude, a series of zigzag switchbacks takes you up over the moraine in a generally northerly direction.

On the Mt. Audubon Trail

Summit of Mt. Audubon in background

Where the trees begin to thin out the route turns west. When you have walked about two miles, a trail junction appears. The trail to the right affords rather a long approach to the Buchanan Pass Trail. But our route goes straight ahead, up across the tundra.

To assure that hikers do not lose their way, huge rock cairns have been built. Some of these are four or five feet tall. As you top the ridge above the trail junction, stop and look off to your right (north) and enjoy the fine view of Meeker and Longs peaks, Pagoda and Chiefs Head, all distinctively shaped mountains in Rocky Mountain National Park. The approach to Buchanan Pass goes up the pretty valley between these peaks and Sawtooth Mountain, where it crosses the Continental Divide. Audubon's summit also becomes visible from this point. After you reach the top of the next ridge, the trail turns south and heads up Audubon's barren ridge, now about a mile and a half away.

From the time that snows recede from this trail until about the end of September are the most enjoyable seasons for this hike. Round trip walking distance amounts to just under nine miles, much of it above timberline and incredibly beautiful.

BUCHANAN PASS

Pennsylvania's James Buchanan, a Democrat who served as our fifteenth President between 1857 and 1861, was the person for whom this remote crossing was named. It was Buchanan who signed a bill on February 28, 1861, that resulted in the creation of Colorado

Territory. Although he never used or even saw
this road, we chose to honor him anyway.

To take this long but beautiful hike, start at
the Middle St. Vrain Recreation area adjacent to
State Highway 160 between Ward and Raymond.
Drive through the campground and park. Although 4-wheel drive vehicles can drive the next
four miles to the trail head, this is a rough, rocky,
and wet route that you will probably prefer to
hike. Originally this was a lumbering road. And
believe it or not, it was once surveyed as a railroad. It follows Middle St. Vrain Creek and runs
about directly west.

Be sure to register at the marked trail head.
Here a footpath leaves the road, turns south
across the creek and starts climbing up through
a tremendous stand of evergreens, passing the
ruins of a large lumbering camp and a genuine
corduroy road. At about two miles from the trail
head this path intersects the trail coming across
from the Mt. Audubon trail, described in that
chapter. Another half mile of the trail will put
you above the timberline. Although wet and
rocky in places, this trail is not steep and the first
mile or so is quite wide and obviously was a con-
tinuation of the logging road.

The jagged peak that now looms above you
directly ahead is Sawtooth Peak, an easy walk-
up from the top of the pass. Several switchbacks
can now be seen crisscrossing the tundra, and
there's even a short cut that should satisfy ex-
hibitionists. The actual top lies in the low saddle
north (right) of Sawtooth. An old weathered sign
marks the 11,837 foot high crest of the Continental Divide. Incidentally, Marshall Sprague

Final above timberline pitch of Buchanan Pass

Jack Morison on the top

View to the west from Buchanan crest

found this pass shown on the old 1899-1907 Nell's Map of Colorado.

From the top the view to the west is far more spectacular than the vista looking east. The water that you see far below you is the south end of the Granby Reservoir. Monarch Lake, the western terminus of this trail, is out of sight behind the peaks. From the trail head, you have now walked about four and a half miles. From the campground the distance is nine miles. This is mainly a summer or early fall hike. Since the trail takes you to the top of the Continental Divide, appropriate clothing is recommended. Weather can change quickly at this exposed elevation.

Looking toward Rollins Pass from Continental Divide

DEVILS THUMB PASS

From a point on U.S. Highway 40 near Frazer, you can look off to the east and see a prominent vertical shaft of rock called the Devils Thumb. The pass that bore the same name was just south of it. In the 19th century it was a pack trail. Some wagons are supposed to have used it. If this was really done, some generalizations concerning the mental state of the drivers would seem to be in order.

You can get to this pass by following Jasper Creek west from Eldora and the site of Hessie to Jasper Lake. Jeeps often make it this far, but it's rugged going. Beyond the lake you can hike to

Old marker on top of Devils Thumb Pass

the top of the pass. Doing it this way you gain nearly 2,000 feet in a mile of walking.

Another, and we think more scenic, route is possible. Drive west from Rollinsville through Tolland and up to the top of bumpy old Rollins Pass. Park near the site of the old town of Corona on top and look for the foot path leading up over the barren tundra to the north. This trail follows the Continental Divide and is to be a part of the proposed Continental Divide Trail system.

Since all of this route is above timberline, observe the usual precautions about electrical storms. The distance from Corona to Devils Thumb Pass is about two and a half miles, and there's a good path all the way. If you stay up on

the top of the divide or close to it, there's almost
no way you can get lost. As you walk north you
can look down on Middle Park at the left. Hide-
away Park, Fraser and Tabernash are clearly
visible far below you. When the weather is nice,
you can see James Peak and the western slopes of
Berthoud Pass on the heights behind you. But
when the weather is bad, you have no business
being up here. Try this one only in mid or late
summer. Be sure to check with the Forest Service to be sure that Rollins Pass is open before
you start up.

DIAMOND LAKE

Diamond Lake's trail is just one more of the
pretty trails in the Indian Peaks area. To get
there, follow the direction given in the Arapaho
Pass or Fourth of July Tunnel Chapters. Follow
the marked trail from the Buckingham
campground toward Arapaho Pass. Go left on the
Fourth of July Tunnel trail and stay on this old
wagon road up to the well-marked trail head for
Diamond Lake.

Here a path turns abruptly south and makes
a couple of creek crossings on logs before it starts
to climb generally back toward the east. The distance from the gate at Buckingham Campground to the Diamond Lake trail head is one
mile. One additional mile of walking will take you
to the lake. In general, this trail is moderately
steep. And there are more exposed tree roots
along this path than you encounter on most
walks, so watch your step, especially if the
ground is wet and slippery.

After you leave the Fourth of July trail, most

Arapaho Peak and path to the lake

Diamond Lake

of this hike is through a dense growth of evergreen trees and is deeply in shade. Just before you reach the lake, the trail opens out into a beautiful example of an Alpine, hanging meadow above 10,000 feet high. John Muir, the great naturalist, once tried to effect adoption of the term "Yosemite" for all hanging meadows. Very few more beautiful examples of this phenomenon can be found. The lake that reposes here is very pretty. Rugged peaks, snow crested even in August, form a spectacular backdrop on three sides. Groves of trees provide shelter while you eat lunch.

All things considered, the brief hike to Diamond Lake is well worth the minimal effort that must be expended in getting there. Try it between early July and mid-October, barring early storms.

FOURTH OF JULY TUNNEL

Nearly every western mining district had a Fourth of July Mine. This one was a silver producer found by C. C. Alvord on July 4, 1872. The lode was sixty feet wide, and its assays varied from $75 to $1,000 to the ton. The trail to the above-timberline mine itself and to the lower tunnel were originally wagon roads. Mostly the mine was worked through the tunnel drilled into the mountainside about five hundred feet directly below the shafthouse. But the ores seemed to diminish, and the property stood idle for more than two decades. Then mining was resumed during the Eldora boom. Later, the mine was "promoted" as a copper producer in a near hoax. No serious mining has been done there since that time.

Pretty path to Fourth of July Tunnel

Surface buildings and dump at end of trail

While in this area, you might be interested in the Arapaho Pass and Arapaho Glacier trails, two very pretty walks that are treated separately elsewhere. To reach the Fourth of July area drive up State Highway 119 to the Eldora Road which turns west from a point just south of Nederland. Go on through Eldora and stay on the road to the Buckingham Campground, just a few miles above the ghost town of Hessie, a parking area is provided in the campground for the trail. Signs and a gate now restrict motorized traffic on this trail. Large water breaks wisely discourage all but foot travel. Shortly after leaving the campground a Forest Service sign on the right directs you to Arapaho Pass. You keep right at this point, left at the next. Farther along, another trail goes off one mile to Diamond Lake. The Fourth of July Tunnel lies just a short way beyond this junction, and the trail ends there. A large dump and several cabins scattered among the trees are all that remain of this historic site except for the above timberline workings, directly above the foot of South Arapaho Peak and reached from the Arapaho Pass Trail. Summer and fall are the best times for taking this hike.

MESA TRAIL

This pleasant low altitude route is usable as a hiking path for almost any season. Start from Boulder's southwestern side and drive up the Baseline Road toward the mountains. Turn left at the western edge of the old Chautauqua grounds and drive south up the hill to the trail head parking area. This is the starting place for both the Royal Arch and Mesa Trails, plus a few others.

The elevation gain on this hike is just about nonexistent, but deceptively so. A wide, well-graded path starts off in a level enough way, but you will soon find yourself walking up and down across a series of moderately steep ridges. The end result is no gain in altitude, but you will do a lot of up and down walking to achieve this objective. Most trails that are as well maintained as this one are also well marked. This trail has beautifully finished signs along the way, but none are at intersections. Most U.S. Forest Service trails are well marked at intersections, where the greatest need exists. But on this one you flip a coin at the trail junctions. If you go for more than a mile without finding a sign, you are probably on the wrong fork.

Some of this trail traverses private land and is heavily posted against motorized vehicles. Specially constructed trail breaks reinforce this restriction. At one point the trail merges its grade with a service road for three quarters of a mile or so before it becomes a path again.

If you want to pursue this trail to its conclusion, a matter of some six easy miles or so, it ends in the town of Eldorado Springs. Quite often people use this as a two car hike, leaving one car at Eldorado Springs to transport the party back to Boulder's Chautauqua grounds. There is no "best" season for the Mesa trail. Barring bad weather it is a pleasant walk at any time of the year. It becomes a good snowshoe trail after a new fall of snow, and it is loaded with a great variety of wild flowers in May and June.

Start of Mesa Trail, near Boulder

Flatirons formations from the Mesa Trail

MITCHELL AND BLUE LAKES

Start from the Mitchell Lake trail head at Brainard Lake, west of Ward, for this beautiful hike among the Indian Peaks. Take the marked, well-defined trail that leads off to the west through a thickly wooded area. In spring and late fall portions of this path are somewhat muddy. And during the insect season the mosquitos are bad here, so carry plenty of insect repellent. Hard winds, common in Boulder County, are very strong up here, so be prepared. But the scenery is just great and well worth these minor inconveniences.

Lots of fairly large, loose rocks, and big tree roots mark this trail. At Mitchell Lake you can compose attractive photographic angles from the east end of the lake. Some people fish here, but we have never seen anything caught. Near the west end of the lake, a sign beside the trail says that Blue Lake is one more mile up the trail. The distance is conservative, and hikers have carved in their own indignant estimates of the real distance. One and a half miles is probably closer, according to our pedometer.

Where the tree growth thins out the trail enters a tundra region. Mt. Audubon is the large, massive, peak on your right (north). No side trails digress from this path, so there's no chance for getting lost. Several large rock cairns make this an easy trail to follow. Where the vegetation grows sparse, practically at timberline, the trail ends at the eastern shore of Blue Lake. For eating a picnic lunch, few prettier places exist. The sharp-topped peak at the lake's western edge is Mt. Toll, named for Roger Toll of the National Park Service.

The path, below Mitchell Lake

Mt. Toll looms above Blue Lake

If you want variety on your return, walk over around the eastern end of Mitchell Lake to the trail that can be seen coming west down off the moraine. This is the lower part of the Mt. Audubon trail and will return you to the same parking lot from which you started. You have now walked barely more than five miles. The best seasons are summer and autumn.

PAWNEE PASS

At various places in this book, several hikes have been described as being among the most beautiful in Colorado. 12,541 foot high Pawnee Pass belongs in this same category. To get there, drive up Colorado State Highways 119 and 72 to Ward. Then turn west to Brainard Lake and drive around it to the parking area for Long Lake and Lake Isabelle. From the western end of the parking lot the trail starts up to the west, generally following the inlet stream between Brainard and Long Lakes. The trail is broad, well planned, and deeply sheltered in a dense growth of evergreens at this point.

A sign at the trail head gives the distance as 4½ miles to the pass. This distance is conservative. Plan on walking about ten miles round trip. A short quarter of a mile brings Long Lake into view between the trees. The trail skirts above its north shore, then makes a series of climbing switchbacks up to the beautiful, subalpine Lake Isabelle. Here the trail divides. A short quarter mile detour to the left goes down to the lake. Our trail goes right to the Pass, posted conservatively here as two miles. Broad, well-planned log bridges cross the streams as the trail continues

Indian Peaks from Pawnee Pass Trail

Marker in wide saddle at the top

to climb. At the only unmarked junction, go left. At timberline you emerge onto a broad tundra meadow with an easy, almost level grade for the next half mile. To the south, Apache and Navajo Peaks make a beautiful backdrop. Mt. Audubon is north of you.

Above the tundra the trail narrows and makes a series of zigzag climbing turns up the rocky talus slope to the west. Actually this is the ridge of the Continental Divide, and when you get to the summit of the low saddle, you are on the top of the pass. If time and weather permit, hike on down the western slope and enjoy a different view. Lake Granby is the large body of water visible in the distance. Or you might plan this as a back pack trip of two or three days, continuing on down past Pawnee, Crater, and Monarch Lakes to U.S. Highway 34 and Granby, both the lakes and the town.

But most people have lunch on the top and then return by the same pleasant trail to Brainard Lake. Best seasons for this one are summer and fall.

ROGERS PASS

Andrew N. Rogers was a Gilpin County mining man who was elected as Central City's mayor in 1873. Rogers was a musician too; the flute was his instrument. He was also an early proponent of a tunnel under James Peak. He first suggested it in 1867. Much later, the Moffat tunnel was created to get the trains from Denver to Salt Lake City, passing under James Peak. This most southerly of the Indian Peaks passes honors the memory of Andrew Rogers. In an earlier day this

Eastern approach to Rogers Pass

crossing was known as South Boulder Pass. Its elevation is 11,925 feet above sea level.

Rogers Pass is a Continental Divide crossing. Its eastern beginning starts near the Moffat Tunnel's east portal, west of Rollinsville. Leave your automobile there, climb over the metal gate at the concrete bridge, and walk toward the trees and the Forest Service sign. There's no mention of Rogers Pass here, but you'll find it listed further up the trail.

On this eastern approach, the path generally follows South Boulder Creek. It is a wet and rocky area and evidence of old corduroy road-building is still very evident. Lush displays of wild flowers grow in the open meadows. In July the Columbine and Indian Paintbrush are abundant here.

Just a short way up, the trail passes some old cabins. Further up, in an open meadow, you will find an assortment of old buildings, all that remains of the early town of Jenkinsville. This was a lumbering community, and was the source of the wood used in construction of the Moffat Tunnel and of many of the railroad ties. At Jenkinsville there's a sign telling you that Rogers Pass is three miles ahead. Distances to Heart and Crater Lakes are also posted.

There are many wet creek crossings before you get above timberline. This is not a well-known trail, and it is not subjected to heavy foot traffic. Consequently the trail is often difficult to follow, particularly at the crossings. Above on the arctic-alpine tundra, the trail switchbacks up above Rogers Pass Lake to the barren but wildly beautiful saddle just north of James Peak, and a "top of the world" vista.

Ute Trail below summit, western side

James Peak from Continental Divide, near the pass

Old marker, top of Rogers Pass

On the western side the route down follows a section of an old Ute Indian trail, running generally northwest. It intersects the Rollins Pass road at the Riflesight Notch trestle and Trestle Picnic Ground. A graded county road generally follows the old railroad grade down to Winter Park, below Berthoud Pass.

If you leave an automobile at each end, this makes a fine two car hike in late summer. But be sure to check in advance about the Rollins Pass road. Sometimes it is closed, even in August. If you go all the way across, the total walking distance is about seven miles. Except for an occasional "unseasonable" year, you should consider Rogers Pass only in late summer, certainly not later than the end of September.

GROUP FOUR

BEAR CREEK TRAIL

This route has nothing to do with the Bear Creek west of Denver, nor does it concern Bear Creek Pass around Sultan Mountain, west of Silverton. Bear Creek, like Clear Creek, has been a popular name for a number of streams in our state.

This Bear Creek Trail is a very old packer route used in pioneer days before Red Mountain and Engineer passes existed. The general destination served was the same, but by different routes. Both climb upward to American Flats, then down the other side to Lake City. It was never wide enough for wagons, only for single-file horse and mule trains. When a less hair-raising wagon road was completed across 12,800 foot high Engineer Pass in 1877, the Bear Creek route fell out of favor.

Start at the tunnel on U.S. 550, the Million Dollar Highway, just a short distance south of Ouray. Park in the wide turnout south of the tunnel on the west side of the road. The trail starts up at the north side of this turnout and climbs up over the top of the tunnel. Originally, it started up from a point about a quarter of a mile

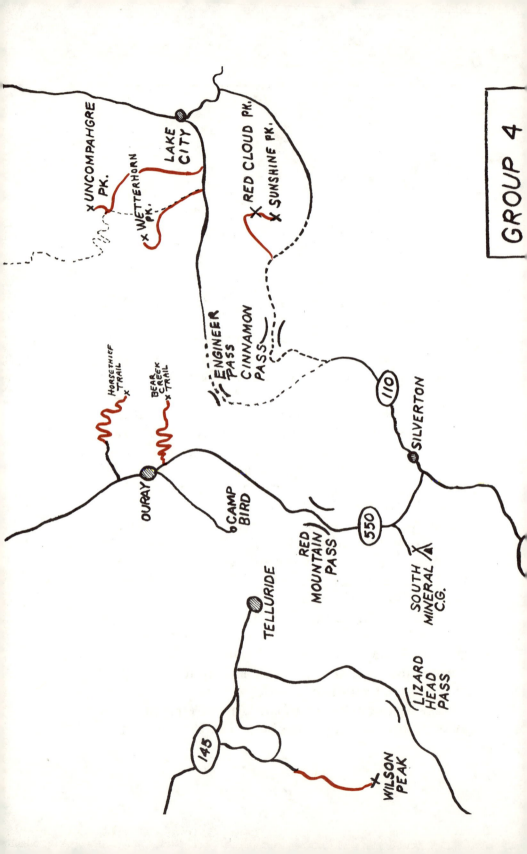

GROUP 4

UNCOMPAHGRE PK. x

x WETTERHORN PK.

LAKE CITY

RED CLOUD PK. x
x SUNSHINE PK.

ENGINEER PASS

CINNAMON PASS

110

SILVERTON

HORSETHIEF TRAIL x

BEAR CREEK TRAIL x

OURAY

CAMP BIRD

550

RED MOUNTAIN PASS

SOUTH MINERAL C.G.

TELLURIDE

LIZARD HEAD PASS

145

WILSON PEAK x

Section of Bear Creek Trail above Ouray

Mt. Abrams from the trail

north. Evidence shows that a pretty obvious landslide dictated a new trail head.

For about the first mile the trail climbs steeply upward across the west face, using a series of zigzag cuts up the sheer rock wall. In one place it crosses a noisy shale rock field. But most of the path is slate, thin but sometimes large pieces. When you come down the trail, walking across this slate sounds like walking on a field of broken glass.

Near the top you get a fine view of White House Mountain, Mt. Abrams, and the Red Mountains. Then the trail turns abruptly east, following a narrow shelf that clings to the sheer wall of the cliff. There are several spots where the trail is nearly gone. By the time you read this, conditions may be worse. A companion, a stout stick, or a rope affords a good feeling of security. Test every step before putting your weight on it. Bear Creek is a long way down below you, straight down!

About three miles of this will show you the best (or worst) of this scenic trail. It really levels out after you turn east, and the elevation gain for this portion is negligible. Picturesque old dead trees, pretty groves of aspens and scrub oak make this an attractive trail for autumn hikes, but it is usually free of snow by early July.

HORSETHIEF TRAIL

During the first half of the 19th century the Spanish and Mexican settlements of northern New Mexico were having a pretty rough time. Far from the mother country, victims of a narrow and indifferent colonial policy that was

Horsethief Trail above Wedge Mine

View from trail overlooking Ouray

Spain's eventual downfall, and denied any metal goods for fear they would make weapons, the people were worse than helpless. Colorado's opportunistic Uncompahgre Utes, ever alert to easy pickings, regularly descended into these upper Rio Grande settlements to steal horses. The animals were sometimes sold in western Colorado but more often in Utah. The route used for moving this purloined merchandise was appropriately called the Horsethief Trail.

Some later accounts insist that the thieves were Americans who stole from New Mexico ranches and sold the horses in the mining camps during the San Juan Silver Rush (1872-1893). Actually the trail is much older than that, and the Ute account is more probably correct. Also since the Utes were very active slave holders and adept slave traders during that era, it seems likely that they would have moved those unfortunate persons over this same route.

Much of the original route, from Lake City, Colorado, to Santa Fe, is now a highway. But there is a fairly extensive section that still remains in its primitive state. Originally it started up the mountainside at the northeast edge of the city of Ouray, but water erosion destroyed this section some years ago. A better approach has been found via Dexter Creek, northeast of Ouray. Drive north on U.S. 550 from Ouray to the Dexter Creek road. Turn east (right) and drive up past the two mines, the Bachelor and Wedge, to the end of the road. The last mile or so is suitable only for 4-wheel drive units, so you may wish to park farther down and walk.

At the end of the road a Forest Service sign

directs you to the trail. It is a fine, wide, well beaten-down trail even today. The grades are modest, and the views of White House Mountain, Potosi Peak, and Mt. Abrams are very rewarding. Then as you go higher, evergreens begin to predominate. Where the trail reaches the top of the ridge and trees become sparse, leave the trail and walk west along the ridge for about a quarter of a mile to enjoy a fantastic birds-eye view of Ouray, cupped in its natural amphitheatre far below.

Up to this point you have walked about two miles. If a short hike is your preference, stop here for lunch and return to town. But you can go on for several more miles of this historic old route. From this saddle it climbs northeast over the ridge and continues along at a generally high altitude all the way to American Flats, near the 4-wheel drive road across Engineer Pass. Along the way you will cross the Bridge of Heaven, a narrow place where you look straight down into fantastic depths far below you. Mt. Sneffels and its handsomely shaped neighboring peaks are in full view from this point. The trail joins the Engineer Pass road near Wild Horse peak on the eastern side.

A better plan for this hike would be to have a friend with a 4-wheel drive unit meet you on American Flats. This is often done. Best time for this hike would be from mid-July until the first heavy snow, probably in October. This is a most beautiful but rather long high altitude hike but well worth the effort.

The San Juans from Red Cloud

Sunshine from Red Cloud

REDCLOUD AND SUNSHINE PEAKS

Years ago, Redcloud Peak's altitude was given at 14,050, but a more recent survey indicates that 14,034 may be more accurate. Sunshine lost a few feet in a reevaluation too. Formerly it was assumed to be 14,018 feet high. Now it is only 14,001 and barely a "fourteener." These two peaks now rank 45th and 53rd highest in Colorado respectively. Redcloud and Sunshine both have a somewhat reddish hue that becomes much more pronounced after a rain. This pigmentation is probably iron oxide.

Start at Lake City and drive fifteen miles southwest on the old Cinnamon Pass approach along the shore of Lake San Cristobal to the site of the old ghost town of Sherman. Turn right here and go on about four more miles to the place where Silver Creek comes down from the northeast to flow into the Lake Fork of the Gunnison River. Here the altitude is about 10,400 feet.

A good footpath parallels Silver Creek, climbing back to the northeast, then south up the slope of Redcloud to the summit. From the river the distance to the top is about five and one-half miles. From here, hike south along the ridge to the summit of Sunshine. Enjoy the view, take pictures and have a bit of lunch before you start back down. There's a shortcut trail back down from the saddle that angles down the ridge to the northwest to join the Silver Creek trail. Go left and follow the path back down to the place where you left your car.

UNCOMPAHGRE PEAK

Deep in the San Juans of southwestern Colorado stands 14,309 foot high Uncompahgre, highest of all the peaks in the most mountainous part of the state. Like Shavano and Tabeguache, this mountain also bears a Ute name. Some translate it as "red lake," while others think it means "hot water spring." The peak itself is a classical geological example of a truncated pyramid, with a huge, nearly flat area on its summit.

There are three routes for climbing Uncompahgre. The first is the most scenic and is by far the longest and probably the least practical. Starting from U.S. 50 east of the town of Cimarron, drive south to the campground and beyond to the sawmill and park your car somewhere out of the way. From here you can backpack in on an old and treacherous trail up the East Fork of Cimarron Creek, an area of incredible beauty. There are towering minarets of pastel colored rocks, tall nearly symmetrical evergreen trees, wispy waterfalls, and the majesty of Wetterhorn and Uncompahgre peaks looming up at the head of the valley.

Jeeps formerly used this road until it was wisely closed off as a part of the Uncompahgre wilderness area a few years ago. We have been told that horses can be rented from the ranch you passed on the road in here from Cimarron. This would be a good possibility since the distance across to Henson Creek is more than twenty miles. Anyway, this road crosses a very old unnamed pass that traverses the range between Uncompahgre and Matterhorn peaks. From the saddle, Uncompahgre's gentle south slope is an easy walk-up.

Uncompahgre Peak from Engineer Mountain

Matterhorn and Wetterhorn Peaks from the flat top of Uncompahgre

The other two routes are far better known, shorter, and very scenic, but lacking in the wild beauty of the route just described. For the first, drive about eleven miles west of Lake City along the Henson Creek trail, which is the approach to old Engineer Pass. At Matterhorn Creek a three mile long trail runs north and then east to the previously described pass at the headwaters of the East Fork of Cimarron Creek. From here a trail runs generally east and then north to the summit.

The last approach is also from Henson Creek, but from a point about five miles west of Lake City. At Nellie Creek a trail turns north, following the creek. Higher up, it angles off to the west, intersecting the route from Matterhorn Creek just below Uncompahgre's southern slope. From here to the top the route is identical to the other two approaches.

From the crest, the view of the San Juan country is a real thriller. As far as the eye can see, tremendous ranges of folded summits stretch off toward the horizon. Coxcomb, Wild Horse and Engineer Mountains present a dramatic panorama. Then turn to face the west for the best view of all, Matterhorn and Wetterhorn peaks, named for two summits in the Swiss Alps that neither particularly resembles. Like a few other places that have been similarly described, this is one of the finest views in Colorado and well worth the effort required to get up here.

WETTERHORN PEAK

Although 14,017 foot high Wetterhorn ranks only 47th among Colorado's above 14,000 foot

Wetterhorn Peak

high peaks, its thin, twisted, upper portion looks more like something out of the Swiss Alps than almost any other mountain in the state. But it really does not resemble the Swiss Wetterhorn, source of its name, in any way. Since it is only three miles west of Uncompahgre, these two peaks are sometimes climbed together, and strong parties have done both on the same day, but an extra day adds to the enjoyment.

From Lake City drive west along the Henson Creek road toward Engineer Pass. At about nine miles or a little over you will arrive at the site of Capitol City, a ghost town which smelter owner George Lee dreamed of making Colorado's capitol. Lee's brick mansion is all gone now, but there are a few cabins west of the site. Turn right

On the approach to the summit

A panorama from the top

here or park your car and hike up to the northwest for two miles to Matterhorn Creek. Now
follow the old trail that parallels north along
Matterhorn peak to the twisting south ridge of
Wetterhorn, now clearly in view. Ascend the
peak by this same south ridge. This is the most
gradual approach, but there's a steep sandy
place near the top where a rope adds a lot to one's
feeling of personal security.

It seems almost superfluous to describe the
grandeur of the panorama you will be able to
enjoy from the top of this mountain, but it's really something. Massive Uncompahgre domi-
nates the eastern skyline. Squarish Coxcomb lies
just off to the northwest and Courthouse and
Chimney are beyond it over toward Owl Creek
Pass. To the south and west are the whole tang-
led masses of the rugged San Juans and Uncom-
pahgres. Be sure to carry plenty of film and, if
possible, wide angle and telephoto lenses with
you. You will probably want to take pictures with
everything you've got.

WILSON PEAK

Despite some published accounts to the con-
trary, neither Mt. Wilson nor 14,017 foot high
Wilson Peak was named for President Woodrow
Wilson. Instead, both mountains were named for
A. D. Wilson, who climbed extensively in Col-
orado Territory when he was here with the
Hayden Survey.

To climb Wilson from the north, drive southeast on State Highway 145 from Placerville toward Telluride. About seven miles down the road
watch for the ruins of a big mill on the left. This

Wilson Peak and Mt. Wilson

San Juan and Uncompahgre ranges from Wilson

A ptarmigan, common above timberline

was the site of the town of Vanadium where uranium was first mined. Turn right or west here on the dirt road that generally follows Big Bear Creek and go about nine miles to the Silver Pick Mine at 11,000 feet.

There are some tricky intersections along the way though. Just over two miles south of Vanadium turn right, to the west. When you have gone about two more miles there is a storage box of fire tools where the road forks into three. Take the middle one and go another two miles to the next junction. Go left or south here for the last five miles to the mine. This final stretch of road is bad. A Volkswagen, a 4-wheel drive or an older car with good clearance will give an added sense of security and safety. Make camp at the mine.

From the campsite, climb slightly southeast to the ridge, then north along the ridge to the top. There is a very striking view awaiting you, so carry plenty of film. Off to the southeast is the rugged and dangerous Lizard Head Peak. To the south are Gladstone and Mt. Wilson. Just west of Mt. Wilson is El Diente. Both of the latter are also "fourteeners" and can be climbed from the Silver Pick campsite.

ଙ

GROUP FIVE

BEAR LAKE TO CUB LAKE

Why not drive up to Rocky Mountain National Park and try this one as an easy seven mile two-car hike? Put one automobile in the Cub Lake Trail parking area, then get into a second and drive up to the Bear Lake parking lot to begin your hike. Start up on the Flattop Mountain Trail which climbs up over the side of the Bierstadt Moraine. At the junction, go right for one and a half miles to pretty little Bierstadt Lake. Then double back to the Mill Creek Trail and drop down along what was obviously an old wagon road to Mill Creek. In general this trail is a shady one. We usually pick a spot for lunch along here.

At one point it traverses an open meadow where four houses used to stand in homestead days, prior to the park's establishment. Only one stone fireplace and chimney remain at present. Now the trail climbs gradually up over an unnamed 8,800 foot high ridge. Just beyond the crest you will intersect the well-known and well-marked Cub Lake Trail. Follow it downhill to Cub Lake. When breaks in the trees occur, stop to enjoy the lovely view up Spruce Canyon. The pond lily filled body of water below you is Cub

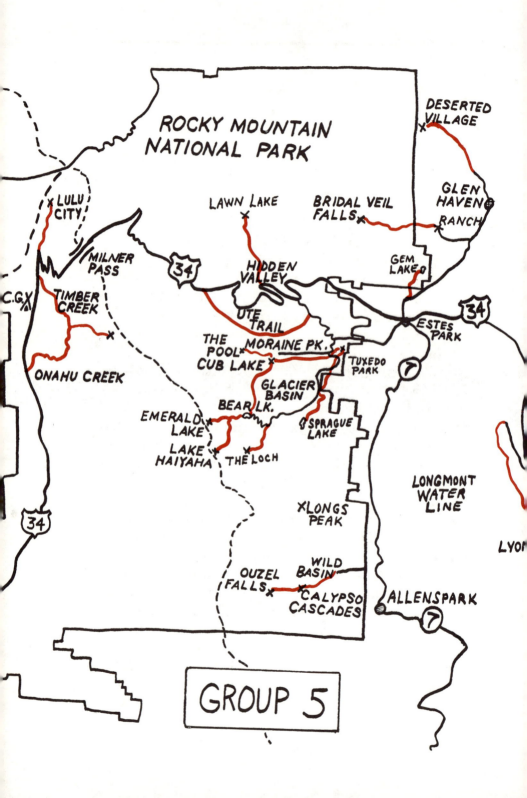

On the trail above Bear Lake

The old homestead site

Lake. From the lake, merely follow the established paths back to the car you placed in the Cub
Lake parking lot. We recommend this trail for
summer and early fall use, depending on mountain weather predictions.

BEAR LAKE TO EMERALD LAKE

Of all of the beautiful trails in Rocky Mountain National Park, this one probably gets the
heaviest summer traffic. In fact, some of this
trail above Bear Lake is paved now. Anyway, it's
a beautiful little walk.

Leave your car at the Bear Lake parking lot
and follow the trail around the north side of
pretty little Nymph Lake. There are five vistas of
Longs Peak from this stretch of the trail. Then a
short walk will put you beside equally attractive
Dream Lake. Dream Lake is longer and the trail
parallels its northern shore. Beyond this point,
the trail follows Tyndall Creek up to Emerald
Lake. There is no trail beyond this point.

Facing the mountains, you will find Hallett
Peak is to the left and Flattop is to the right of
the lake. Tyndall Glacier lies between these
peaks along the headwall of the Continental Divide. The round-trip distance to Emerald Lake
and back to the trail head is just under four miles
of extremely nice scenery. Although summer is
the prime time for this trail, many of the natives
prefer hiking it in the autumn after the "people
season" is over.

Looking across the lake toward Hallett Peak

BEAR LAKE TO THE POOL

This is another two-car hike within Rocky Mountain National Park. Begin by putting one car in the parking lot beside the Fern Lake Trail head in Moraine Park. Then get into the second vehicle and drive up to the Bear Lake parking lot. From this point, start up the Flattop Trail. When you reach the junction, go left toward Flattop Mountain, climbing up over the Bierstadt Moraine, one of the best examples extant of a lateral moraine. At the next junction, take the right trail toward Lake Helene and Odessa Lake.

As you climb, there are good but distant views of Lake Bierstadt and Longs Peak. The trail's high point crosses a rocky saddle north of Flattop

Longs Peak looms dimly above the trail

Mountain and east of Notchtop Mountain. Lake Helene can be seen below just after you cross the crest. Some of the finest scenery can be seen now as the trail begins its descent down Odessa Gorge. The trail itself is on the west slope of Joe Mills Mountain above the gorge. A wide, shady spot in the trail just below Little Matterhorn Peak makes a very pretty lunch stop.

As it continues to lose elevation, the trail now passes around Odessa and Fern Lakes. Old patrol cabins are visible around the shore of the latter. Beyond the cabins the trail crosses Fern Creek and generally parallels its course down to Spruce Creek, dropping sharply down to the Pool.

Here the path descends Odessa Gorge

From here a well-defined trail, sometimes called the Fern Lake Trail, leads out to the picnic ground trail head where you left that first car.

Total elapsed mileage of this walk is about nine miles of good firm trail, neither excessively rocky nor sandy. Due to the altitude around Lake Helene, however, snow flurries may be encountered in July and August, and patches of snow are found here and there most any time. This is a particularly scenic hike through quite varied terrain that is not difficult in any way. Grades are gradual if you start at Bear Lake, steep if you begin from the other end, and that nine miles is total.

BRIDAL VEIL FALLS

From Estes Park Village, drive northeast on U.S. Highway 34 toward Glen Haven. Turn west on the graded road to the McGraw Ranch and park by the west edge of the ranch on this side of the fence. The trail runs west along Cow Creek and is a double rut ranch road at this point. It soon narrows into a path and enters Rocky Mountain National Park. A small sign marks the boundary.

The elevation gain is most gradual, only about 1200 feet in the entire two and a half miles to the falls. Total round trip distance is about five miles. About a mile and a half beyond the ranch the trail forks. A left branch goes east up Black Canyon. Our trail goes right and follows Cow

Near the start of the trail

Bridal Veil in winter

Creek along the base of Sheep Mountain, crossing the stream several times. In general, this
trail is a well protected one, nestled down in a
valley. Most of it is heavily wooded, but there are
a few open meadows near the beginning.

At the falls the trail ends quite abruptly. In
early winter these falls are quite beautiful, with
a sheer wall of textured ice cascading vertically
down into the valley. Later in winter, the trail is
too easily lost and snow drifts are sloped in the
wrong direction for snowshoeing. But in spring
and fall, this is a pretty hike. Several good places
to eat a picnic lunch can be found when you reach
the falls.

Due to a change in ownership of McGraw
Ranch, the Park Service is now negotiating a
new access to this trail. Inquire at park head-
quarters before attempting this hike.

Cub Lake and the Pool

Although each of these two places can be
treated as a separate hike, we put them together
since several of the other recommended hikes in
Rocky Mountain National Park utilize parts of
these trails. We prefer starting at the trail head
for Cub Lake because it is easier to walk down
the trail between the lake and the Pool than to
climb back up it. Simply follow the pleasant,
well-marked trail for the two miles or so to the
lake. Early in the morning on quiet days, it's not
unusual to find elk along this trail. In summer,
very pretty wild flowers are most abundant here.
There are a number of small-to-medium sized
bodies of water along this trail. Don't mistake
them for Cub Lake.

On the Cub Lake Trail in autumn

Lily pads in Cub Lake

After following the base of the valley for most of the way, the trail enters a dense and quite pretty grove of aspen trees, then it climbs sharply up to Cub Lake. Profuse pond lilies make this a very pretty spot in late summer. The trail parallels the north edge of the lake and gradually gains elevation up to the point where the Mill Creek Trail comes in from the left. This is just about the highest elevation on this trail. Now the trail loses altitude fast by traversing a heavily wooded hillside below Spruce Canyon.

From the Pool, merely follow the pretty lake trail almost straight east to the parking area, then walk along the narrow graded car road to the Cub Lake parking lot where you parked before starting up the trail. Summer and autumn are this trail's best seasons. In winter, either trail individually can be good for snowshoeing from the trail heads up but do not try to go over the top. Total walking distance is just over six miles with 1000 feet of elevation gain.

CUB LAKE TO TUXEDO PARK

This is another of the many short hikes one may take in Rocky Mountain National Park. Park your automobile at the start of the Cub Lake Trail, cross the footbridge and begin walking south along the regular trail. Then at the place where the trail forks, go left across Moraine Park, cross the river and hike along the level south edge of the park. Soon this trail becomes a dirt road. Follow the road almost to the cluster of cabins, then look for the footpath that begins climbing up among the cabins to the southeast. This will carry you up on top of the

View near Cub Lake Trail junction

High point of trail above Tuxedo Park

South Lateral Moraine to an elevation of about 8,800 feet.

Where the trail comes out at the eastern end of the Moraine is a good lunch stop. At this point, walk out to the edge and look down on the highway. Across from you and a bit to the left, the irregular rock formation is "Teddy's Teeth," named for Theodore Roosevelt, the only conservationist ever to live in the White House. Off to your right, the cluster of red-roofed buildings is the Y.M.C.A. Camp of the Rockies.

From here on you can follow the trail on down the hill to Tuxedo Park. An automobile left at that end of the trail helps. Or you can just turn around on top at the end of the Moraine and head back for the Cub Lake trail head. We prefer summer and fall for this walk.

DESERTED VILLAGE

The Fourth Earl of Dunraven was an Irish millionaire and so-called sportsman. In the mid 1870s he tried to acquire the whole of Estes Park to be used as his private hunting preserve. But keeping trespassers out proved impossible and Dunraven disposed of his vast holdings in 1907.

This hike's destination may have been used as one of his wilderness hunting camps. Louisa Arps and Eleanor Kingery, co-authors of the invaluable *High Country Names*, feel that His Lordship's lodge was probably a bit upstream from the Cheley Boy's Camp, perhaps in the corral or beyond. The cabins now known as Deserted Village are probably the remains of a resort run by Fred and Alta Spragne. It was still operating as late as 1909.

Bridge on Deserted Village Trail

Cabin and ruins of the village

To get there go north out of Estes Park on the Devils Gulch Road through Glen Haven following North Fork of Big Thompson Road to sign "the Retreat." Turn sharply left, cross the creek and drive to trail head. This is a narrow dirt road, rough, dusty, and single laned but not dangerous. The trail head is downstream from the Trails End Ranch. It would be somewhat shorter to come out of Loveland on U.S. 34 to Drake. Then take North Fork of Big Tompson Road six miles to the Retreat sign.

From the trail head the path goes up to a ridge, then it starts down the steep trail to the river. Turn right at the river and go upstream. This first quarter of a mile down to the North Fork of the Big Thompson River is the steepest part of the hike. You will pass the Cheley Camp and on a warm day their stables have a way of making their presence known. Flies are quite bad there.

Some rather attractive rustic bridges are found along the additional two miles to the village, and the river is not far away at any point. At the edge of the open meadow that contains Deserted Village, a small footbridge will get you across the river. The trail goes on to a pretty grove of trees that makes a pleasant picnic stop. The cabins near the water, shown in the accompanying picture, and some other nearby foundations are all that remain of the Deserted Village.

If you follow the trail on beyond the cabins it will take you to the boundary of Rocky Mountain National Park in about one additional mile, but the trail is both rough and somewhat steep.

Except for a few places that are obvious, most of the trail that you have followed up here from the trail head may have been Lord Dunraven's wagon road. In bringing supplies up here the wagons were heavily loaded, and at times His Lordship was in the same condition. Generally speaking, this is a very good trail, has easy grades, wanders in and out of the shade throughout most of its length, and there's something to see when you get there. Summer and early fall are the most desirable times for visiting the Deserted Village. Some people from Fort Collins regard it as a pleasant snowshoe trip. Total walking distance is about five miles.

GEM LAKE

This trail, like the one to Bridal Veil Falls, is another of those short but delightful hikes found along the outer perimeter of Rocky Mountain National Park. Start at the first traffic light at the eastern end of Estes Park Village. Begin driving up the road toward the Stanley Hotel. Turn right onto the Devil's Gulch Road at the first major intersection. Stay on the pavement and follow this road around to the trail head for Gem Lake. A U.S. Forest Service sign on the left side of the road marks the trail head, and a small parking area is available. For the first quarter mile or so the path runs between two fences, turns right, then abruptly left.

Soon after you leave the fences behind, the path becomes a gently climbing trail, well graded and clearly defined. There are a few moderately steep inclines but it's mostly an easy grade, sheltered by tremendous stands of evergreen trees.

Gem Lake Trail, Longs Peak in background

Gem Lake in early winter

Occasional openings permit rather attractive views of Prospect Mountain and Longs Peak. At one place there's an unusual boulder with a head-size "hole in the rock" opening that has some picture possibilities.

Up higher the trail makes a series of climbing switchbacks as you near the top of Lumpy Ridge. Then there's a spectacular view as the trail opens out just short of the lake. Elaborate rock cribbing holds the trail up at this point. Then you round a corner to enter a massive cove, protected by high rock walls. Ahead of you in this secluded bowl a sandy beach surrounds Gem Lake. Down at the far end, conveniently out of sight, are two rest rooms. Near the lake, several big tree trunks provide a good place to sit and have lunch while enjoying the view. Total hiking distance, round trip, is just under four miles with about 1000 feet of elevation gain. Summer and fall are the best times for this little expedition. In many ways this is a good trail for children, or for the novice hiker who lacks experience, or for the person lacking time, who just wants to take a short hike where there's pretty scenery.

GLACIER BASIN TO SPRAGUE LAKE

Enter Rocky Mountain National Park at Beaver Meadows. Take the Bear Lake Road to Glacier Basin Campground and park there. Walk up the hill at the eastern edge of the campground to get on the Glacier Creek trail. Follow it in a generally southwest direction, gaining some altitude as you cross an 8,697 foot high ridge. Where the trail levels out on the other (western) side, cross the creek and proceed along to the "Livery" sign.

Go right (north) on this fine trail that quickly becomes much wider, obviously an old wagon road. This leads directly to the Sprague Lake area with its lovely picnic ground, a fine spot for lunch.

Abner Sprague arrived in Colorado in 1864. Eleven years later he defied Lord Dunraven by filing a claim in Moraine Park, later Steads Ranch. On a later land acquisition here in Glacier Basin he put up a hotel and created this beautiful lake. When the Park Service acquired his land they tore the hotel down.

A delightful little trail circles Sprague Lake, revealing many picnic spots and good picture possibilities looking west across the lake toward Flattop Mountain, Otis and Hallett Peaks. After lunch, take the unmarked trail leading northeast from the northwest end of the lake. Follow it to the point where it disappears into a body of water of modest size. Look straight across and familiarize yourself with the terrain where the trail starts again on the other shore. Then pick your way carefully around the end of the lake, to your right as you face the water. Step on the larger tufts of grass and don't be surprised if you get your boots wet.

When you are back on firm ground, look for the pipe that carries water to the Glacier Basin Campground. In a general way, the path back to your car follows this pipe. The total walking distance for this trail is between four and five miles, depending on the amount of hiking you do around the lake. The elevation gain and loss is negligible, making this a very easy, rather sheltered, and quite pretty hike.

Hallett Peak and Sprague Lake

LAKE HAIYAHA

Lake Haiyaha and its trail are two of the real beauty spots of Rocky Mountain National Park. Start at the Bear Lake parking lot and follow the well-marked trail around the southern shore of that lake. Go on past Nymph Lake. Just before you reach the eastern end of Dream Lake, watch for a junction in the trail. Go left at this fork and continue climbing up around the exposed southern shoulder of an unnamed hill. Pause now and then to enjoy the scenery. The square topped peak off to your left is Longs. Just below the lake you will cross Chaos Creek, a pretty little rill that originated up in the saddle of the Continental Divide between Hallet and Otis peaks. At the

Lake Haiyaha

Hallett Peak and trail to the lake

lake, numerous gnarled trees around its shore enhance picture possibilities at this unusual site.

As you start back, watch for an unmarked footpath that drops off the side to the southeast. This is one of the older trails, no longer used now and not shown on current maps. We were over this with friends once some years ago. After a couple of tricky intersections it puts you on the upper part of the Glacier Creek trail near the Glacier Gorge Junction parking area. A left turn here will let you hike back up to the starting point at Bear Lake. Total hiking distance is a bit over two miles each way. Try this one in summer or fall.

Lawn Lake Trail

LAWN LAKE

This is another of the Rocky Mountain National Park trails. Enter the park at the Fall River station and drive west to Horseshoe Park, past Sheep Lakes to the picnic ground just east of Roaring River. The trail begins here at an elevation of 8,626 feet. It follows Roaring River back up the canyon, gaining altitude gradually. Several species of rather pretty wild flowers are found along this trail.

The grades are quite gradual and most of the trail lies shrouded in thick stands of aspen and evergreen trees. This is not the most scenic trail in the park. It is pretty but not spectacular. No really majestic mountain panoramas are seen.

The lake is a lovely spot though, nestled in a 10,987 foot high bowl between Mummy and Fairchild Mountains. Two patrol cabins were built along its eastern shore to shelter those who make it this far. One of these burned in 1964 and has not been replaced. The second cabin was razed by the Park Service. Summer and early autumn are the best seasons for this rather long trek.

THE LOCH

Several trails have been described within these pages as being among the most beautiful in Rocky Mountain National Park. It would be difficult to choose among them; fortunately such a choice is unnecessary — enjoy them all. This is one such hike. You can start from the eastern end of Bear Lake or from Glacier Gorge Junction. Most persons prefer the latter. The trail runs south, then southwest around the two glacier knobs, gaining altitude gradually. Many lovely views are found as you walk along. Be sure to carry a camera with you.

In season, pretty wild flowers are found along this trail. The Loch is a lovely middle-sized lake, nestled in a secluded basin between Otis Peak and Thatchtop Mountain. Its elevation is just under 10,000 feet. We think this is one of the most scenic lunch stops in the park. If time and weather permit, follow the path on around the lake's north shore and on up to the smaller Glass Lake and Sky Pond, in icy Loch Vale. The distance to the Loch is about two miles. The remaining trek to Sky Pond is just a bit over a mile.

Of course this trail is best in summer, but it's

Longs Peak and foot path to the Loch

The Loch

also nice in the fall when the first snows have started to blanket the high peaks.

LONGMONTS WATER LINE

This is a somewhat unusual trail, a one-of-a-kind. On this walk you'll hardly ever be out of sight of paved highway, yet you'll be far above it. Start at Lyons and drive northwest on State Highway 66 toward Estes Park; turn west off this road onto graded county highway and follow the stream up to the small dam and headgate on the right side of the road. Almost across the road from the dam you will see a narrow grade that heads back down the canyon, more or less paralleling the road you came up on. This is the beginning of the trail.

The narrow Water Line path

It wanders around, following the contours of the mountains, working its way down toward Lyons. At one point where it seems to stop, look for the grade on the hillside to your left and walk across to it. Where the trail appears to end at an abrupt rock wall, you can stop for lunch and retrace your steps back to the car, or you can climb up over the obstruction. The trail resumes again on the other side and goes down to Lyons. By the time you reach the rocky obstruction you will have covered just over two miles. Barring bad weather, this trail is good from May (watch out for ticks) through October.

At this writing a gate has been placed across the access road to this trail as described above. But the trail can still be entered from the Longmont Power Station at Lyons with permission of the caretaker. This involves a scramble up the pipe line — quite steep but short.

LULU CITY

This is a fairly short and quite easy hike to an old ghost town site in the western half of Rocky Mountain National Park. The trail starts at the old Phantom Ranch site, where Trail Ridge Road makes an abrupt switchback to the southeast as it begins the climb to Milner Pass.

Park in the picnic ground adjacent to the trail head. The walking distance each way is under three miles. Although there are a few little hills to go up and down, most of this trail is pretty level, and very well defined. It follows the valley of the North Fork of the Colorado River. Where the trail climbs up east of the river, this is only to avoid a swampy section on the original trail.

On the old wagon road to Lulu City

Almost empty site of Lulu City

The abandoned cabins in Shipler Park belonged to an early-day cowboy-prospector known by the unlikely name of Squeaky Bob. Just before you reach Lulu City, the La Poudre Pass trail takes off to the right. At Lulu City, only old foundations remain. At the south end of the townsite, walk back southeast toward the river to see the old bear trap, often used as the town jail.

Lulu City was founded on a hoax by Benjamin Franklin Burnett, who named it and a nearby pass for his daughter, Lulu. When it was found that the gold really wasn't there in paying quantities, the whole boom collapsed.

If the weather is warm and time permits, you could go on up the trail to Lulu Pass, now called Thunder Pass. A sign at the upper end of the town points the way and tells the three mile distance. You might prefer bringing a sleeping bag and making this a two-day jaunt. Your return is by the same route. Summer and fall are the best times for this walk.

ONAHU CREEK

On the western slope of Rocky Mountain National Park, just south of the Timber Creek Campground, is the trail head for Onahu Creek. At the start, the trail is quite sheltered, nestled deep in a dense evergreen forest. All of the grades are gradual, and there's a lot of rapid gain and loss of elevation. For most of its length, the trail follows the valley of Onahu Creek, but does not necessarily parallel it at all times.

About a mile and a half above the trail head there's a fork. Both branches proceed somewhat northeast and join the Timber Creek Trail, which

The bridge over Onahu Creek

in turn runs north through Long Meadows to
join up with the Timber Lake Trail. Partly because of its sheltered nature, this tends to be a
rather wet trail. Perhaps this explains why, in
season, it has what must be the worst mosquito
infestation in the park. And yet this wetness
produces benefits too. Rare red columbine and
calypso orchids grow along this trail.

This is a well graded and quite pretty trail,
but not in the usual sense. There are few places
along it where you can see out through the trees
to view surrounding mountains. But the lush
growth of ferns and unusual wild flowers make a
hike up this trail worthwhile. Round trip distance up to the Timber Creek Trail and return is

about five miles. The elevation gain is roughly 1,400 feet.

OUZEL FALLS

Down in the southeastern corner of Rocky Mountain National Park there are several quite pretty little trails. One of them goes to Ouzel Falls. To get there take Colorado Highway 7 to Allenspark, then north to Copeland Lake. Turn west around the lake, go on to the Wild Basin Campground and park. The trail leads west along the north bank of North St. Vrain Creek to Calypso Cascades.

Here the Allenspark Wild Basin trail comes in from your left. From here continue on along the Thunder Lake Trail for a short distance, about

The bridge near Ouzel Falls

one mile, to Ouzel Falls. Most of this trail lies deeply shrouded in a dense growth of evergreen trees. Two quite attractive rustic bridges span the creek at Calypso Cascades and at Ouzel Falls. There are attractive picnic spots on the creek banks above and below the latter bridge.

If you have the time and equipment for overnight camping, you can continue on up the Thunder Lake Trail to the shelter cabin near the eastern end of Thunder Lake, but this involves several more miles of walking. The round trip distance to Ouzel Falls and return is under four miles. While summer is probably the best season for this hike, its altitude is low enough to permit its use well into Autumn.

TIMBER LAKE TRAIL

This trail begins on the western slope of Rocky Mountain National Park at a point just a mile or so north of the Timber Creek Campground. A parking area has been provided on the east side of the road and signs direct you to the start of the trail. In the opinion of experienced hikers, the posted mileage to Timber Lake is conservative. Plan on walking at least a mile more than the distance that is posted at this writing.

Some Park Service employees will admit to these discrepancies privately, but not for publication. Some years ago the late Sen. Harry Byrd staged a personal vendetta on these signs and read some of the wilder ones into the Congressional Record. Our Park Service people do a wonderful job under difficult conditions, and we should probably forgive this annoyance.

Timber Lake is a beautiful trail, with breath-

A sheltered section of the trail

Bull Elk, below the lake

taking panoramas of the Never Summer Range. Most of the trail is heavily timbered, but there are breaks in the trees and the views are marvelous. The trail wanders around the southern slope of Jackstraw Mountain, at times paralleling Timber Creek. Then it climbs up into a high open meadow at about 10,800 feet elevation. Wild flowers bloom in profusion here. At the northeastern end of the clearing, the trail gets swampy and turns off to the south.

Here the trees grow thickly as the trail begins a final ascent to Timber Lake, now less than a mile away. The largest, finest, bull-elk we have ever seen was encountered in a pretty clearing on this final section of this trail.

Although this is a rather lengthy walk, it is a particularly pretty one and there's something to see when you reach the end. If you plan to do this in one day, start early, plan on lunch at the lake at 1:00 p.m., and remember that walking downhill always takes less time. Summer, from the last week in June through the first week or so in September, would be the preferred time.

TUXEDO PARK TO GLACIER CREEK

Although we have used this trail primarily as a five mile round trip snowshoe route, obviously it can also be used as a summer and autumn hiking path.

Enter Rocky Mountain National Park at the Beaver Meadows station, then turn left at the first intersection onto the Bear Lake Road. Just after you cross the Thompson River by way of the concrete bridge, the road bends right into Tuxedo Park. Leave your automobile near the trail

Snowshoe trail to Glacier Creek

head sign. The trail starts off to the south, skirting the edge of the Y.M.C.A. stables. Since this trail is somewhat difficult to follow in winter, it would probably be wise to familiarize yourself with the terrain in summer.

Gradually the grade gains altitude, but you never get above Timberline on this one. Where the trail winds around the southern slope of Emerald Mountain, the snow piles in at quite a steep angle, making walking a side hill proposition. Apart from this one section, this tends to be a pleasant trail. After crossing the ridge, you will be going downhill all the way to the Glacier Basin Campground. Although closed in winter, you enter this campground from the back. It makes a pretty good spot for a winter picnic. When returning, just after you recross the ridge, notice the rough profile on Rams Horn Mountain. This ridge is called Teddy's Teeth and was named for Theodore Roosevelt. Best seasons for this one would be anytime except spring.

UTE TRAIL

Actually there are many Ute trails in Colorado, and most are not connected. One is encountered on a mountain top near Evergreen. Another goes up from the Turkey Creek area to South Park. There's also a place to get onto the Ute Trail in the Garden of the Gods, near Colorado Springs, and there's another near Salida. Since all of them, and some others, bear the same name, one might logically wish for more variety in assigning names.

Perhaps the most scenic of all is the Ute Trail that crosses Rocky Mountain National Park in a generally northeast to southwest direction. In fact, it was this same Ute Trail that gave the name to Trail Ridge Road. If desired, you can get onto it at the Milner Pass parking area. It follows the western slope terrain traversed by Trail Ridge Road in a rather general way over Fall River and Iceberg Passes. It crosses the main highway just below the Forest Canyon Overlook and comes through the Ranger Station buildings above Hidden Valley, more than 11,000 feet high. Since this area is all above timberline, watch for the cairns that mark the trail. Cairns are piles of rocks, stacked one atop the other. Because this trail is much less used than most others in the park, it is advisable to get the next cairns in sight before leaving the previous one. During the mining period this trail was used by prospectors crossing the range to Lulu City, Dutchtown, and Gaskill. Athough records show some wagons were used, pack trains of mules and horses seem more likely choices.

We think that this trail makes a particularly attractive two car hike. Leave the first car at the end of the dirt road that ends by Beaver Brook, in Beaver Meadows, between Beaver and Deer Mountains. Then drive the second car up Trail Ridge Road to the Ranger Station (stone buildings on the north side of the road) beyond Rainbow Curve, cross the road and pick up the trail on the south side. It wanders off to the southeast just under Tombstone Ridge.

At Timberline Pass, 11,484 feet high and unmarked, you have reached the highest point on this part of the trail. Stop here and get your bearings. The first mountain on your left is an unnamed summit on Tombstone Ridge. The next is Beaver Mountain and that first car you parked in now in a straight line to the east of you below Beaver Mountain. The swampy area way down below you is Moraine Park. The edge of Estes Park village can be seen to the east, also a corner of Lake Estes. Longs Peak is clearly visible to the southeast. To the left of it are the Twin Sisters with a fire lookout on the top. Below them, the red-roofed building complex is the Y.M.C.A. Camp of the Rockies.

From this point on down, it would be better to have someone along who has been over this trail. The trail down not only becomes indistinct, it is nonexistent in some spots. In general it goes

Along the poorly marked Ute Trail

Timberline Pass, the highest point

along a rough and steep grade through Windy Gulch, where it becomes pretty well defined again and easy to follow. Then it winds across the southeast shoulder of Beaver Mountain. From there it goes across into Beaver Meadows and to the trail head. You should be able to see your car from between the trees on Beaver Mountain and sort of chart your course from there.

On our first exposure to this trail we made the mistake of crossing through the low saddle between Beaver Mountain and Tombstone Ridge. This gets you into some pretty rough country and necessitates hours and hours of uncomfortable sidehill bushwhacking. If this happens, locate the profile of the square-topped Deer Mountain to the east and head for it. Before you get there you must cross Beaver Meadows and will probably see your car. Anyway, this is a very beautiful hike. The total distance, if you use two cars, is about eight miles. And the unobstructed mountain panoramas are just great. Be sure to carry a camera. To be safest, try the Ute Trail only in summer. Autumn is a "maybe" thing at this elevation. Since Trail Ridge is often closed on Labor Day, forget this trail after that time.

GROUP SIX

MT. COLUMBIA

Before you start on this one be sure to purchase a copy of the U.S. Geological Survey quadrangle map, the 15 minute series, Mt. Harvard quadrangle. The rather complicated access route is shown very clearly on this fine map. Two words of caution should be observed from the beginning. Parts of the so-called road to be described get maintained only erratically. If county bulldozers have been in recently you may sail right through without any problems. But it depends on when you happen to go as apparently no regular maintenance schedule exists. Consequently, you may encounter conditions that will cause you to take our names in vain. Older cars with more clearance, 4-wheel drive, or a Volkswagen work best.

Anyway, to parallel and supplement the map, here are the instructions for reaching Mt. Columbia. From the light at the main intersection in Buena Vista, drive north for four miles on U.S. 24 toward Leadville and Granite. At about the northern end of the town watch for a county road that turns west or left. It may or may not be marked. Vandals seem to have concluded that nice dry highway signs make dandy firewood and

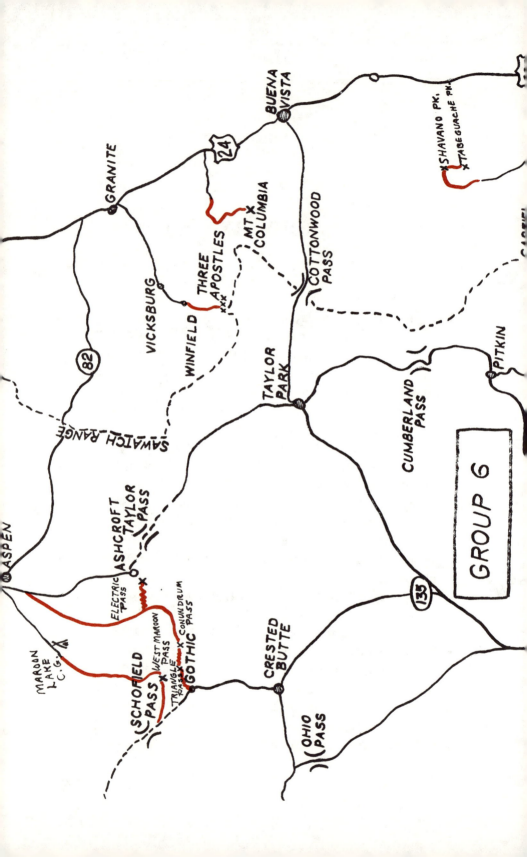

On the trail, near timberline

the intersections on this little-used road may or may not be marked when you go.

Drive west on this county road for two miles, then north and west for one additional mile. Now the road turns south on a washboard type, somewhat unpleasant road for five miles, paralleling North Cottonwood Creek. Pass the marker for the Main Range Trail and go on to the marked (we hope) parking area where the road stops.

Put on your pack here and start walking west to a marked junction, less than two miles. Don't go toward Kroenke Lake, go right on the Horn Fork Trail. There's a good camping spot up here before you get to Bear Lake where you can spend the night below timberline in a quite pleasant open meadow.

View from the summit

Marshall Brown on the top

Mt. Columbia's trail starts from this campsite and goes east up a grassy slope for three miles to the 14,073 foot summit of the peak. If the weather is good and your party is so inclined, Colorado's third highest peak, 14,420 foot Mt. Harvard can also be climbed from this valley.

CONUNDRUM AND TRIANGLE PASSES

Although one source lists the altitude of this crossing as 12,300, the sign on the top says 13,059. According to Len Shoemaker who built many fine trails in Western Colorado during his long tenure with the U.S. Forest Service, the unusual name of this pass goes way back into the mining period. Gold seekers who found good float there were never able to locate the lode that was the source. One of the baffled argonauts said that it was a "conundrum." So, for lack of a more plausible account, the pass was named.

To see this old crossing drive south from Aspen on the Ashcroft-Castle Creek road for five miles to Conundrum Creek. You are now twelve miles from the pass. The first half dozen miles of the Conundrum Creek Trail is best negotiated in a 4-wheel drive vehicle. The rest of it is in a wilderness area and must be hiked. A hot spring, bearing the same name as the pass, is also a puzzler. It will be found just before you start up the pass. By the time the summit is achieved you will be a long way back in from civilization. So sit down, have your lunch, and enjoy the rugged scenery. The western descent into Chicago Basin and East Maroon Creek is precipitous. Be very sure of what you want to do before you start down. Prospectors went this way to reach the rich Chicago Mine.

Top of Conundrum Pass

Summit of Triangle Pass

You might consider instead planning this as a two car outing. From the top of Conundrum Pass there is another trail that runs west along the ridge to Triangle Pass. Its other side drops down Copper Creek, past Copper Lake, to the ghost town of Gothic, easily accessible from Crested Butte by car. The distance down to Gothic is about seven miles. This whole trek is a rather long and strenuous one, but it affords the person willing to walk the extra distance with a rich opportunity to study nature in a magnificent unspoiled wilderness.

ELECTRIC PASS

Although this pass is 13,200 feet high, it was nevertheless an old mining trail and was used in the 1880s. In those days it was called the Panorama trail or the Pine Creek Prospector Trail. Burro pack trains used it to pack rich gold ore down from Michigan ridge, past Cathedral Lake, to the Castle Peak smelter at Ashcroft, which was bigger than Aspen at that time. Ashcroft is now one of Colorado's best-known ghost towns.

Electric Pass crosses the range that separates the Castle and Conundrum Creek Valleys. Len Shoemaker surveyed and rebuilt this trail for the Forest Service in the 1920s. He also named it after being knocked down three times by an electric storm. He escaped by rolling down the slope and lived to tell about it after three days of recovering in bed. As a result a previously undesignated pass got a name. The trail already had a name, but the pass it crossed did not until this incident. Electrical storms are very

Approaching Electric Pass on tallus slope

Top of Electric Pass

common on this ridge and were first noted by the F. V. Hayden survey party in the 1870s.

Electric Pass is accessible from both sides of the range. Using directions given in the Conundrum Pass chapter, you can follow the Conundrum Creek trail from five miles south of Aspen. After you have hiked about one and one-half miles in from the Wilderness boundary the Electric Pass trail junction will be found at approximately 10,200 feet altitude. It begins climbing up to the east, using a series of zigzag cuts to gain elevation. You will cross Cataract Creek before you reach the ridge and the old sign that marks the top of the pass. From the junction to the top is just over three miles.

But there is an easier approach from the east. Drive south from Aspen on the paved Ashcroft-Castle Creek road. Turn right beyond Ashcroft and park at the Pine Creek Campground. Hike west along Pine Creek on the well established trail past Cathedral Lake to the pass. Although steep in places, this is the more beautiful of the two approaches. This route is sometimes used as a horseback trail. It also makes a fine two car hike, with a vehicle placed at each end.

SHAVANO AND TABEGUACHE PEAKS

Colorado's Rockies contain a number of unusually shaped mountains, some of which have profiles that resemble something other than just a rocky peak. Snow formations give others a distinctive appearance. Mt. Ypsilon and Mt. of the Holy Cross are examples of the latter. Chiefs Head, Teakettle Peak and Sleeping Ute Mountain are typical of the former. And when a peak

Mts. Tabeguache, Shavano and the Angel

boasts some of these unusual characteristics, it usually means that legend makers have been busy or will soon produce stories to explain why this or that mountain looks as it does.

But of all the legendary mountains in this state few have been as richly embellished by story-tellers as 14,229 foot high Mt. Shavano. Its claim to legendary status comes from a snow formation on its eastern slope that resembles a broad-hipped female figure with arms stretched upward. The figure is visible in June and has usually melted off by the first of July. In the most interesting of the several early stories the snowy form represents a Ute Indian maiden named Corntassel who gave her life to assure her people

Near the false summit

View from Mt. Shavano

a good harvest. Her annual appearance heralded a promising crop when the Utes resided on the Western slope. More recently the figure has become known as the Angel of Shavano, although she has no wings. Needless to say there are plenty of Angel legends.

Actually, Mt. Shavano was named for a Tabeguache Ute war chief who, curiously, led his people in the ways of peace. Just a mile away down the ridge is Tabeguache Mountain, 14,155 feet high. Usually, both of these peaks are climbed together.

To get to the place from which one may ascend these two summits, drive northwest from U.S. Highway 50 at Maysville to the Shavano campground. If you are some distance from home spend the night here. Then go on to Jennings Creek, less than two miles further up the road. Begin climbing to the north on the trail that parallels the creek. Head up toward the steep burned-over slope, clearly visible from the road below. The trail turns east to the crest of Tabeguache. There is a small herd of mountain sheep up here, watch for them.

There's a 500 foot drop in the saddle between Tabeguache and Shavano, just a mile away, and the ridge route is obvious. From the top the view across the upper Arkansas Valley is stimulating. To the north is Mt. Antero, and if the day is clear you can see Mt. Princeton beyond it.

On your return stay on the west side of Shavano and contour back across McCoy Gulch to the Jennings Creek trail and return to your car. By the time you return you will have walked about eight miles and, counting the saddle, the total elevation gain was 4,200 feet.

Three Apostles Peaks and the trail

THREE APOSTLES TRAIL

This trail is considerably more remote and not nearly as well-known as most others in this book. To get there drive north from Buena Vista or south from Leadville on U.S. Highway 24. Just south of Granite, turn west at the Clear Creek Reservoir and drive thirteen miles on this graded road through Vicksburg to the old ghost town of Winfield, turn south and cross the creek at the west edge of town.

Weather conditions during the previous few days will determine how far you can drive on this road. It soon degenerates to a trail and then proceeds to get worse. Its end is in a bog across the meadow from the ghost town of Hamilton. Using

a 4-wheel drive vehicle, we have been able to
drive all the way on two occasions. From the end
of the "road," start walking straight ahead,
south, on the path through the willows. It soon
becomes a firm trail and progresses on up the
valley.

Since this is neither a well-known nor a
much-traveled hiking path, the route becomes
indistinct at several points. Where the trail
stops, bear slightly to your right and keep the
Three Apostles Peaks on your left. When you
reach the above-timberline tundra, start looking
around to get your bearings.

The huge peak down near the start of this
trail is Mt. Huron, one of our above 14,000 foot

The dim path above Hamilton

high summits. If you are in doubt on your return,
head for Huron. While you are up here, look for
the lakes. There are at least two quite large lakes
up here on the tundra. And there are fish in
them. But in common with most high altitude
fishing, the results can be either sensational or
awful. Be prepared for either. When you have
hiked as far as you care to go, merely retrace
your steps.

The average round-trip distance will be about
six miles. July, August, and early September are
the preferred months for this one.

WEST MAROON PASS

Altitudes of 12,400 and 12,500 feet have been
given for this old prospectors' trail that was
pioneered in the 1880s. The difference is hardly
worth fussing about. Miners from Scofield
(Schofield) City and from the Lead King Basin
area used this crossing in the 1880s for access to
Ashcroft and Aspen. It crosses a high ridge south
of the treacherous Maroon Bells, separating
West Maroon Creek from the Crystal River
drainage. It was the Hayden Survey party that
first planted the name "Maroon" which now appears on three peaks, two passes, a creek, a lake,
and a very pretty campground.

Drive southwest from Aspen to the Maroon
Campground, or you can park in the Maroon
Lake parking area. Hike southwest on the trail
past Crater Lake. Here the path turns abruptly
south following West Maroon Creek up toward
the pass. Total distance from your car to the top
is about sixteen miles.

This too can be a two car hike if arrangements

have been made to leave a second vehicle at one of the wider places on the north side of Schofield Pass. The distance from the top of the pass down to the Scofield road is under four miles of very wild and beautiful country. Particularly after a rain, the maroon-red hues of the surrounding mountains present a breath-taking panorama.

Maroon Lake and the Maroon Bells

The top of the pass is well marked

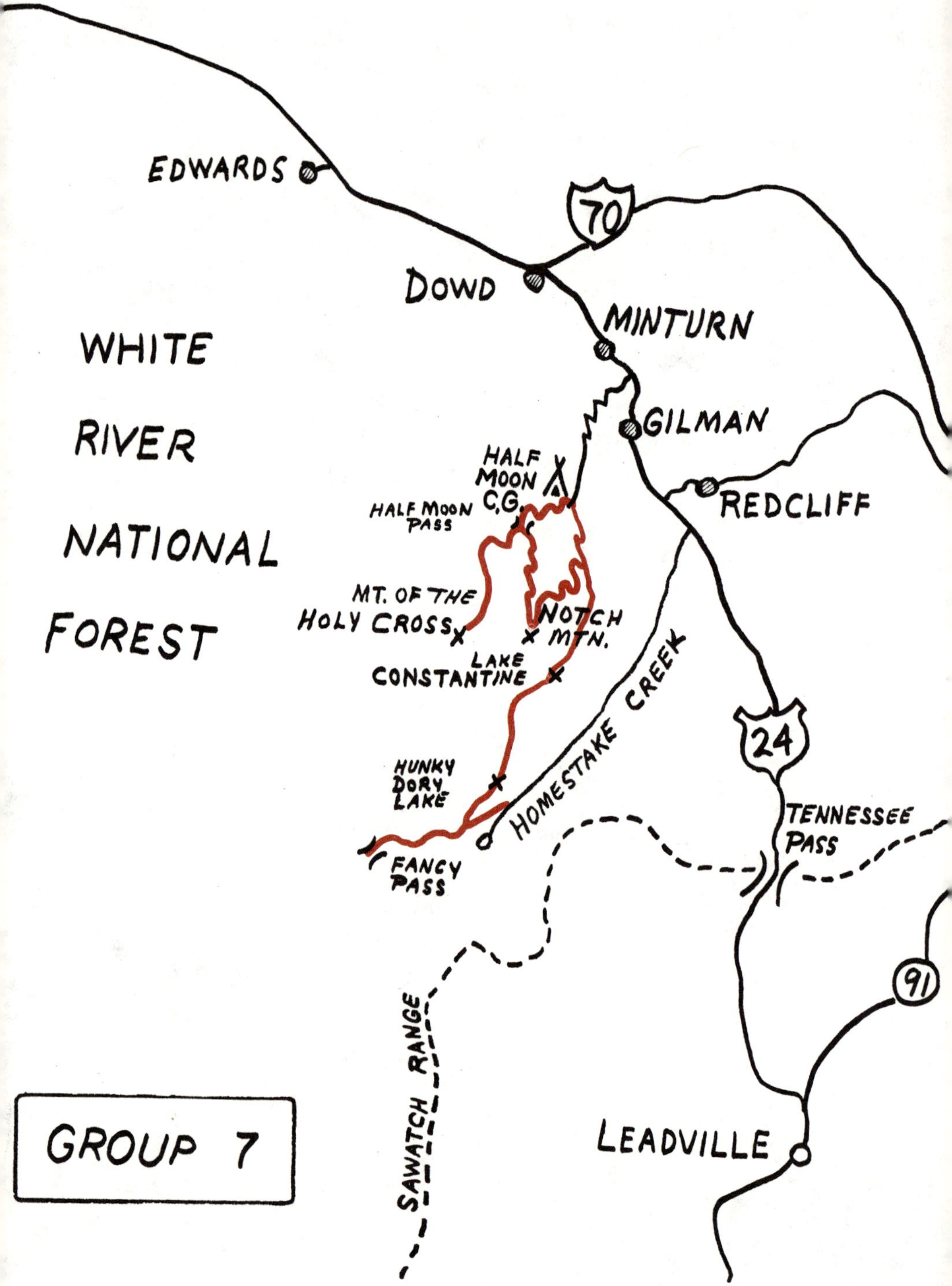

EDWARDS

70

DOWD

MINTURN

GILMAN

WHITE

RIVER

REDCLIFF

NATIONAL

HALF MOON C.G.

HALF MOON PASS

FOREST

MT. OF THE HOLY CROSS ✗

NOTCH MTN. ✗

LAKE CONSTANTINE ✗

HOMESTAKE CREEK

24

HUNKY DORY LAKE ✗

TENNESSEE PASS

FANCY PASS

91

SAWATCH RANGE

LEADVILLE

GROUP 7

ᘒ

GROUP SEVEN

FANCY PASS

It's a long and somewhat tiring twelve mile round trip up to Fancy Pass and return. But it's a rather historic hike too, and it will take you to one of the more obscure historic places in Colorado. Joseph W. Fancy, a miner in the now-defunct Holy Cross district, was the source of the pass. It was built by the Treasure Vault Mining Company when they wanted to get their mill into Holy Cross City. The rival Gold Park Milling and Mining Company had denied them the use of their road, which was the only route to the town at that time.

Start at Red Cliff and drive south toward Leadville on U.S. 24. Before you reach Pando, turn off to the southwest, past the campground, then go on up along Homestake Creek to Gold Park. Here you start on foot up the old four mile mining road to Holy Cross City. If you have a Jeep-type vehicle you can probably drive up to Holy Cross City, we have lots of times. But there are other times when this is not possible. This is a rather rugged road, with huge rock ledges, bogs, and steep grades. The distance to the old town is four miles, and after examining the road, you may prefer to walk.

East side approach to Fancy Pass

In any case, when you reach the empty cabins of Holy Cross City, go left where the trail forks. No matter what you are driving, park it here and walk the last two miles to Fancy Pass. The trail is impossible for anything except hikers and mules. As you climb higher, stay up on the ridge, don't go down to the lake if Fancy Pass is your destination. Much of this part of the grade is rocky and above timberline. The top is recognizable by a huge rock cleft and an ancient, battered sign. The summit elevation is 11,550 feet. If the weather looks at all inclement, this is no place to be. We have seen snow at Holy Cross City in August, although it doesn't last very long. Be sure to take adequate clothing and extra food in

Sign at top of the pass

this country. In short, for most enjoyable conditions, try this one only in summer.

HALF MOON PASS

U.S. Highway 24 leaves U.S. 6 and Interstate 70 at Dowd to follow the Eagle River Valley south toward Tennessee Pass. Just below Dowd is the little village of Minturn. Two miles south of Minturn a graded road leaves the paved highway, going right near an old mill. This road makes many loops and curves as it climbs up Bishop Gulch to the Tigiwon Campground. Further up this road is the somewhat higher Half Moon Campground. If you plan on staying overnight, stay at Tigiwon. The mosquitoes are awful at Half Moon.

Anyway, the road ends at Half Moon Campground, and there's a small parking area where the road stops. Two trails start from this point. One crosses the creek and heads for Notch Mountain. The other goes straight up the hill and leads to Half Moon Pass. At the first junction, almost in sight of your car, keep left. The Pass is two miles ahead on this path. For most of the way you will be sheltered by a dense growth of evergreen and aspen trees. But as you near the top the trail breaks out into a clearing, affording an awe-inspiring panoramic view of the Gore Range behind you.

At the top the view of the closer Sawatch Range is every bit as good. As you face this latter range, the massive peak to your left is Notch Mountain. If Notch were not there, you could see the Mt. of the Holy Cross from this point. You can hike up the ridge of Notch to see it from the top,

Trail on east side of the pass

Summit, Half Moon Pass

but there's a dim trail which is a boulder-hopping proposition.

If you continue on over Half Moon Pass for about a half mile or so, the trail rounds a point from which you get a northern view of Holy Cross, but the cruciform of snow is not visible from this angle. If you go on down this trail it will lead you to East Cross Creek, a shelter cabin, and the point from which people climb Holy Cross. Try this hike anytime from June through September as the weather permits.

LAKE CONSTANTINE AND HUNKY DORY LAKE

For this very beautiful hike, use the same instructions for reaching the trail head as for Mt. of the Holy Cross or Notch Mountain. At the Half Moon Campground, above Minturn, park in the designated area, cross the creek, and walk east, then south on the Holy Cross Mountain Trail, paralleling Notch Mountain Creek.

This is an excellent trail, well marked and easy to follow. Where it forks, you go straight ahead. The right branch goes to the top of Notch Mountain. From this trail division on to the lake your route stays generally in timber. You will have walked approximately four miles when you arrive at Lake Constantine. Here you can make a decision to go on up to Fall Creek Pass or to return to the car. The distance is another two and a half miles to the pass.

Beyond Fall Creek Pass the trail turns west and then south down past Seven Sisters Lakes, then slightly southeast to Hunky Dory Lake, a gem-like body of water at timberline. At times the fishing is sensational here. Since the entire

Trail to Lake Constantine

Lake Constantine

Hunky Dory Lake

distance from Half Moon Campground has been nine miles, you might like to consider an alternative.

From Gold Park, on Homestake Creek southwest of Red Cliff, a "hairy" 4-wheel drive road goes up to Holy Cross City. Where this trail crosses French Creek, a branch trail runs northwest to Hunky Dory Lake. With the right sort of vehicle, this could be a sensational two car hike.

Depending on the weather, anytime after the last of June through mid-September would be the preferred times for this unusually pretty hike.

MT. OF THE HOLY CROSS

Although Holy Cross is not one of our highest 14,000 foot peaks, about fifty others are higher, it usually takes two days to pack in, climb to its 14,005 foot summit, and get back out again. Unless you are a very fast climber, be sure to take a warm jacket, sleeping bag, food, etc., with you. For the first two miles, follow the instructions given in the Half Moon Pass chapter. Cross the pass and start down the steep trail to East Cross Creek, losing practically all of the elevation gained up to this point.

At the foot of this trail, beside the creek, an old prospector's cabin still has a tight roof and you can sleep here. Next morning you should cross the stream on the logs just below the cabin and get an early start up the trail. Aside from a few logs that you will need to climb over or walk around, this is a pretty good trail, but you can't see much from it until you reach timberline.

Photo by Charles Grover

Mt. of the Holy Cross

Here we usually tie something visible on a tree to help mark where this part of the trail reenters the forest when you come back down. To us there's a peculiar sameness about this particular place and some sort of marker helps.

Above the tree line, there is a tundra path of sorts here and there, if you can find it. The next obstacle is that big rounded shoulder to the south. This is the northern extrusion of Holy Cross. Once you are upon it, walk generally uphill toward the summit, now in full view. Stay away from the snow to your left. High winds undercut the snow on this ridge, creating deep cornices that break off in July and August. The actual summit is quite rocky, so just pick the

Marshall Brown on summit of Holy Cross

easiest route for yourself. Be sure to sign the register when you reach the top, then sit down to enjoy the view.

To the east, above Notch Mountain, the light colored patch is the Climax dump on Fremont Pass. The Gore and Tenmile Ranges loom up prominently too. Over by South Park are the Mosquitoes, dominated by Lincoln and Democrat, near Fairplay. Behind you to the west is Mount Jackson, and far away you can see the Maroon Bells, Capital, Pyramid and Snowmass, all "fourteeners."

If you get off the summit by noon, most people can make it back to the car at Half Moon before dark without too much strain. An easy but steady pace is probably best. July and August are the best months for this most scenic and very rewarding climb.

NOTCH MOUNTAIN

For this particular hike, there are two possibilities, because Notch has two summits. Both provide magnificent views of the Mt. of the Holy Cross, and both start at the Half Moon Campground. Follow instructions from the Half Moon Pass chapter to get to the trail head, then go up to the saddle of Half Moon Pass. But instead of following the trail down over the side, walk to your left toward Notch Mountain. Stay with the trail on the left or east side of it.

Where the trail ends, it's a boulder-hopping proposition to the top, now in full view. This is the spot from which William H. Jackson took his most famous photograph of Mt. of the Holy Cross in the 1870s. A rock cairn marks the summit and the

On the pretty path up Notch Mountain

Mt. of the Holy Cross from Notch Mountain

view from here on a clear day is one of the finest in Colorado. Just south of the summit is the notch. Don't try to cross it to the other summit. The grade is incredibly sheer.

Meanwhile, back at the Half Moon Campground, take the trail marked Notch Mountain, six miles. It takes you to the other side of the notch. Although longer, this is a much better trail and affords a different but equally awe-inspiring view of Holy Cross. There is only one fork in this trail and the correct route is clearly marked. Much of this latter trail lies shrouded in a thick evergreen forest, but the last three miles or so are above timberline. When you reach the above 13,000 foot high summit, a fine stone shelter house provides a welcome resting place. From here the face of Holy Cross seems even closer than from the other crest.

Many people arrange in advance with the ranger at Minturn to spend the night up here. The return from either side of Notch Mountain is by the same route. For best results and best pictures, try this hike between June 15th and September 15th. If inclement weather seems imminent, wait for another day. Electrical storms on the top of Notch are as incredible as the view on a clear day.

❧

GROUP EIGHT

CRAG CREST TRAIL

In our opinion, the Crag Crest trail is one of the prettiest and most satisfying hikes in Colorado. It may have been an old Ute Indian trail, but evidence is inconclusive and opinions vary. It starts on Grand Mesa in the National Forest south of Mesa and north of Cedaredge. Drive to the Crag Crest Campground on Eggleston Lake. The trail begins just behind campsite No. 2 or from the parking area just below it. It is a very well defined and maintained path as it starts off generally toward the northeast. Most of this part is in the shade of tall evergreens, and a most abundant growth of wild flowers blankets the meadowlands on either side of the trail.

Little Eggleston Lake, about three-fourths of a mile from the starting point, is the first landmark. Trout seem to be most abundant here. Beyond the lake is Reservoir No. 1, at a distance of one and one-half miles from the trail head. Just beyond the reservoir the trail divides. The trail going left leads to Butts Lake and is quite short. Your trail goes up across the boulder field and into the trees again. Until you reach timberline the insects can be bad through here. Next, the trail crosses an expanse of volcanic rock and

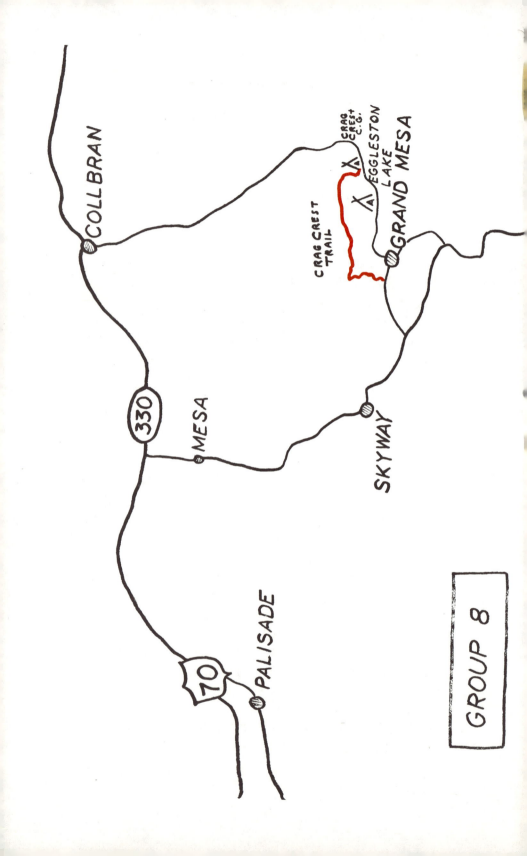

Trail above Little Eggleston Lake

Rocky section of the trail near the top

you get a fine view of the San Juan Mountains far to the southwest and of the Grand Valley. For the next hundred yards or so the trail again enters the trees and remains in the shade until it reaches the crest of the ridge. There is an unbelievably fine view in all directions.

In general the path now follows the craggy crest of the ridge for some distance. Gradually the elevation gained is lost as the trail drops down to emerge on Colorado State Highway 65 near the northeast end of Island Lake. Total distance of this trail is about six miles. This trail is a good one for a two car shuttle, leaving a vehicle at either end. Barring this, the hike to the top of the ridge and back to the campground is most pleasant and not too strenuous. Considering the elevation and exposure to the elements one encounters on this trail, summer is the best season.